Miracle Messenger

April,
 Life is eternal
Imagine the possibilities!

 Love &
 Light,
  Virginia

"This book is the ultimate proof of life after death. Following the passing of the author's son in 2006, she and her family received hundreds of after-death communications from him—ongoing interaction, dream visitations, orbs, hummingbird appearances, etc. If you have any doubt about our survival of death, this book will dispel it."

—Tony Stubbs, author of *An Ascension Handbook, Living with Soul, The Other Side* and *Death without Fear*

"If you want to reap the rewards of unconditional love, inspire hope and belief in reunion with your deceased loved one, this is the book to read. You will surely learn that all life is connected, you can forever have a relationship with your loved one, and learn to grow in the process."

—Dr. Louis LaGrand Ph.D., Author, world-renown researcher on After-Death Communication phenomena, former professor emeritus at State Unversity New York

"I send kudos to Shelly for providing this sweet and touching book. It reinforces the need that we make spirit contact to receive wisdom from the other side, a pure truth void of the distortions of ego, selfishness or dogma."

—Albert Clayton Gaulden, Author and Founding Director of the Sedona Intensive

Miracle Messenger

Signs from Above
Love from Beyond

Virginia Michelle "Shelly" Hummel

A family's remarkable account
of life after death

Copyright 2011 by Virginia Michelle Hummel

All rights exclusively reserved. No part of this book may be reproduced or translated into any language or utilized in any form or by any means, electronic or mechanical, including photocopying, recording or by any information storage and retrieval system, without permission in writing from the publisher.

StarChild10 Publications
Palm Desert, California

Hummel, Virginia Michelle "Shelly"
Miracle Messenger: Signs from Above, Love from Beyond
Virginia Michelle Hummel; Foreword by Albert Gaulden

First StarChild10 Publications paperback edition December 2011

ISBN 987-0-9834787-0-6
Library of Congress Cataloguing-in-Publication Data 2011905056

Copy Editor: John Carrigan, CarriganCommunications.com
Post-Copy Editor: Carol Adler, write-to-publish-for-profit.com
Cover photo of hummingbird: Dean Mayo, foretography.com
Cover/interior design: Mark Anderson, Aquazebra.com

AQUAZEBRA™

Disclaimer and Reader Agreement

Under no circumstances will the publisher, StarChild10 Publications, or author be liable to any person or business entity for any direct, indirect, special, incidental, consequential, or other damages based on any use of this book or any other source to which it refers, including, without limitation, any lost profits, business interruption, or loss of programs or information.

Persons mentioned in this book have given their permission to the author to use their names.

We live with the illusion that we are separate from each other, God, and the Universe, when in fact we are all a drop in the same bucket.
VMH

Christopher William Arrington
June 19, 1980 -

Acknowledgments

Because I believe we are always guided by spirit when we listen, I would like to express my deep gratitude to God, Chris, my angels and guides for helping me in the creation of this book.

From the moment I asked for the right people to be put in my path on March 7, 2011 to take a partial manuscript and a rough idea through to fruition in just over a month, everything fell into place.

Thank you to my daughter, Kristin, for being brave enough to share some of your most painful and private experiences with Chris. Olivia, thank you for your understanding, especially for having to go without a home cooked dinner for a month while I completed the manuscript. Thank you both for your love and support always.

Peter, thank you for all that you have done for my children over the years and for what you continue to do for Logan. I am so very grateful.

Mom, thank you for *always* being there for me and my children.

To Chris Adams who knows me better than anybody. Thank you for listening without judgment to all my stories as they happened, for your support and advice when I was hurting and for holding me when I needed to cry. You are the best kind of friend.

Mandi and Barbara, words cannot express my gratitude for loving my son and being such a big part of his life.

For Vicki Mills, a kindred spirit: Thank you for your advice and guidance through this project.

To Dolores Carruthers, a friend and mother who has also lost a son: Thank you for your words of wisdom and watching out for my best interest.

John Carrigan: Thank you for the valiant effort you put forth to edit as fast as I could write.

Thank you, Mark E. Anderson for making my vision of the cover and my book a reality.

Carol Adler: When I needed a fresh set of eyes, Spirit dropped you in my lap. You read my mind. Thank you.

Pam: Thank you for sharing your story with me and for allowing my girls to spend time with your beautiful Silver. We miss him.

Thank you, Albert Clayton Gaulden, Author and Founding Director of the Sedona Intensive, for your lovely words about my son. Your program changed our lives.

I would like to thank Dean Mayo for his generous donation of the cover photo of the Hummingbird. Dean is a PGA Professional and a photographer. Please visit his website at foretography.com to view his extraordinary pictures.

Thank you, Vicki Petrick, talented interior designer, who among other things suggested the perfect spot in my house to sit and write.

And last of all: Thank you, Dad, for believing in me.

Contents

Foreword 1

Note From The Author 5

1 The Journey Begins 7
Introducing Shelly, Chris, Kristin, Olivia, Uncle Peter,
Mandi, Barbara, Samantha & Logan

2 Shelly's Story
    The Knowing... 21
    "52" 22
    Premonition 24
    And He Shall Prepare The Way 25

3 Uncle Peter's Story
    Father's Day In Cancun 31
    Room 420 35

4 Kristin's Story
    Three Friends 39

5 Pam's Story
    Reality TV 43

6 Mandi's Story
    Friends Forever 47
    Can You Hear Me Now? 52

7 Barbara's Story
    Little Light Of Mine 57

8 Shelly's Story
    Manifestation 59
    Hello From Heaven 62
    You Light Up My Life 64
    Kuan Yin 65
    "Hi" In The Clouds 69
    Take Me In Your Arms 72
    Hummingbird 73
    Just A Quick Hello 75

9 Mandi's Story
    Special Delivery 77
    Hug Me Hello 77

10 Shelly's Story
    Out Of The Mouth Of Babes 79
    A Nudge From Spirit 80
    Over The Rainbow 85
    Answered Prayers 87

11 Kristin's Story
    Do You Get It Now? 91
    Heavenly Hands 93

12 Shelly's Story
    Golden Light Of Love 95
    All Aboard 97

Keep Your Eyes On The Road 98
I See The Light 99
Ask And You Shall Receive 102
Be Careful What You Ask For 106
Give Me A Sign 107
What Spirit Wants 109

13 Mandi's Story
The Power Of Prayer 113

14 Olivia's Story
Hide & Seek 117
Talk'n To Grandpa 119
Circle Of Friends 120

15 Barbara's Story
On The Wings Of Love 121

16 Shelly's Story
Happy Valentine's Day 125

17 Kristin's Story
Oh Child Of Mine 131

We Are Not Alone 139

About The Author 143

Bibliography 145

Foreword

When Chris Arrington's mother, Shelly, asked me to write a Foreword for *Miracle Messenger* I signed on with pleasure. Chris changed lives even when this observer felt people were trying to change his. It is eerie to reflect on what he taught me and others around him here in Sedona when, at nineteen, he went through my personal growth program, the Sedona Intensive.

I met Chris through his Uncle Peter whose reflections are in this book. Peter is one of the most caring, loving and sharing souls I have ever met. To know Peter is to know he embraces the thunder of silence, and Chris learned this from Peter. When there was a need, Uncle Peter was there to offer support. In fact, Peter did a lot to make a difference in many lives within the family circle and beyond.

My business partner, Scott Carney remembers Chris teaching him how to juggle when Chris stayed in Scott's Intensive client lodge. Later it was revealed to Scott that Chris was trying to teach him about balance and about keeping his eyes on all the balls in the air that he had to handle in his life.

Chris was silent when I wanted him to roar responses to the sense-activators in which I tried to engage him, in order to clear him of the traumas and chaos that I felt were running through his body and soul circuitry. I learned from Chris what Joel Goldsmith, the founder of The Infinite Way, tried to teach me in his masterful book, *The Thunder of Silence*. I learned about a wordless world where "Consciousness Shift" happens when you hit the "mute" button. In other words, I came to believe that Chris came to see me and my support team because he needed to give and he needed to take away the essence of caring and sharing, of connecting with those he knew and those he would know.

What is true for me is that Chris lives on and he sends messages to family and friends as he did to me at the time of his transition. The reason many cannot hear him when he speaks is because they cannot hear. As the Hopi Indian instructs us, "Keep your ear to the ground to hear what you need to know." To this day Chris still says a lot of things to me that I need to know.

Shelly's book underlines the notion that those who appear to be dead are actually more alive than those of us still on the earth plane. They are just in another compartment of life. I refer to where Chris is, as *the perfect place*. I distinguish that "here" is the earth and "there" is the Other Side of Life. It is my opinion that we view transition from this dimension to that one as a time of grief and loss. His family knows he is happy where he is and he speaks to those who can hear. I send kudos to Shelly for providing this sweet and touching book. It reinforces the need that we make spirit contact to receive wisdom from the other side, a pure truth void of the distortions of ego, selfishness or dogma.

Perhaps Chris made his transition from here to there in divine order. Perhaps Chris knew there was going to be a lot of confusion and torturous times on earth, and that he was called to a higher assignment: one that would clarify the marvelous resolution of what Earth's pain and suffering were all about. When you understand the powerful influence he still has on his mother, uncle and sisters, and many,

many friends, you can rejoice in the evolution of the soul.

From time to time Chris calls to me and I answer. It is comforting to know that everything he came to teach me I am finally learning; and for that I am very grateful. God bless you, Chris Arrington. You are an angel of illumination.

—Albert Clayton Gaulden, Author and
Founding Director of the Sedona Intensive

Note From The Author

Losing a child is one of the most painful experiences we can have, and recovery seems impossible. We question ourselves and our beliefs. We question almost everything about our life, and we ask why—why did it happen and why did it happen to us? What did we do wrong?

With the questions come the regrets and so many other feelings that we soon discover are part of the grieving process. In time, if we are patient with ourselves, we also come to understand that the questions and feelings of loss are given to us as an opportunity from which we can grow.

In 2006 when my son, Christopher was killed in a motorcycle accident, I chose to stand in grace. I knew I must honor him by being the best I could be and by having unwavering faith in God. I vowed to help others through the inevitable darkness that falls when a child crosses over.

Shortly after Chris made his transition, several of those close to him came to realize that he had not left, after all. Often he would contact us to remind us of his presence. There is so much more to life than we have been led to believe, and Chris has been one of our best instructors.

The following book is a collection of our experiences with Chris since his death. It is my sincere wish that these stories in some small way will lighten your heart and ease your pain so that you too, can embrace the possibilities of life after death and discover the infinite way of eternal love.

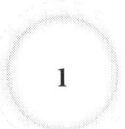

The Journey Begins

**Samantha, Logan, Chris, Kristin, Shelly, Olivia
Christmas 2000, Reno, NV**

When I was eight years old I stood alone in my parents' driveway and stared at a brilliant blue sky, cloudless, perfect. I can remember that moment as if it were yesterday—the heat of the asphalt beneath my sneakers, the sweet smell of freshly mowed grass, the colorful array of mid-summer blooms from my mother's garden.

Yet, with all the beauty of nature around me, a vague sense of sadness swirled through my heart. I felt abandoned, lost, set adrift to find my way alone.

It was a cruel joke someone had played on me. I had no

idea who I was or what I was doing here. I had the *knowing* that I'd been given specific instructions—ones I had agreed to undertake—but as I stared at my empty hands I knew I had failed before I had begun. Had I taken notes? If so, where were they?

I vaguely recall a list of things to do and the specific reasons why they must be done, but I had no idea what they were.

I pinched my arm. I was here all right. My flesh was warm and firm, but my mind cried with confusion. With no memory of this body or this place with its unfamiliar people, I felt no connection, no recognition. I had the distinct feeling I was on the outside looking in. Surely there must have been a mistake.

Someone had to know what my confusion was all about, and the only person I could think who might help me was God. So I asked him.

Right there in the middle of my driveway, I asked, "Father, tell me why I'm here." It seemed like a simple question, straightforward and honest, that certainly deserved a straightforward, honest answer.

I closed my eyes and listened intently, certain I would hear His voice.

I heard nothing except the gentle rustle of leaves on the apple trees in our front yard.

Maybe He didn't hear me.

I asked again.

I felt so small in the encompassing silence, waiting for an answer, fearful it would never come. Then, when I could stand it no longer as I strained to hear above the far-off din of the highway, the occasional bark of a dog and incessant buzz of the bees as they gathered nectar from my mother's flowers, I begged, promised, and pleaded for Him to answer me.

Beneath my tears and soft sobs, beneath the fear that consumed me at the thought of having to stumble along in this world without guidance was the reality that maybe this was it. Maybe there wasn't any more and I was alone.

It was disappointing not to hear a voice or a thunderbolt—not to see a neon sign lowered from the sky with a message telling me why I was here and what I was supposed to be doing. After all, if He really was up there, He would answer me, wouldn't He? It seemed reasonable.

I knew I couldn't ask my parents these philosophical questions because they would have absolutely no idea what I was talking about. I'd get some mumbo jumbo about birds and bees and babies and we're supposed to go to college and get married and have a family and die in a rocking chair on a front porch. That seemed a little too simple, considering the magnitude of what I was contemplating.

You'd think at eight I would have had more childlike ambitions on my mind, like mastering a skateboard or pogo stick! What child in their right mind would even ponder such serious questions?

Christopher William Arrington arrived on June 19, 1980, eighteen months after the birth of his brother, Rett. I was twenty-one years old. With no ambition to have a career outside the home, I longed to have a family I could call my own.

I had helped my parents raise my two younger

brothers, Peter and Stephen, and their innocence, love and wonder inspired me. I felt at ease in their presence and could never figure out why the world wasn't filled with love and kindness.

As a child I would watch life unfold around me and cringe at the hurtful things that were said or done to each family member in my household. I could never remember a time when I saw my parents hug or kiss in a deep and meaningful way.

Actually, I could never figure out why they got married in the first place. As a child I had a memory of a kinder, gentler place and was at a loss to understand how I ended up here in this family—in this world—where human life was not celebrated as the precious thing it was meant to be.

Christopher was a gentle, loving soul with a beautiful smile that radiated from within. His big dark eyes and blond hair beckoned me to love him with every ounce of my being. And I did. At twenty-one, however, I was still a child myself, and unaware of the wisdom, restraint and self-discipline needed to raise a precious, innocent human being.

Although I did the best I could at the time, I would give anything to change what I did wrong, to give Chris the undivided attention he deserved, and be a mother he could truly count on at all times.

These truths are unbearably painful and made even more so by the fact that he is gone. I have no way to right these wrongs, no chance at redemption. My hell is here on earth, living daily with the knowledge of exactly what I would have chosen to do differently.

When Chris was six months old, my marriage fell apart and Chris' father and I divorced. We were too young to have been married in the first place. With two babies at home, I was exhausted at the end of the day. My husband was trying to make a living and not particularly interested in raising a family. After working all day he wanted to come home to a wife who could set aside the babies and pay attention to him.

He wanted to ski on the weekends and continue his college life style. We were not on the same page and after I discovered he'd had an affair, I realized I could no longer trust him.

Chris had yet to form an attachment with his father, and when he came for his weekend visits I would only let my older son go with him. It was painful for me to watch Rett's father drive away with my little boy. He had little interest in either child; I felt his visits were solely for the benefit of his parents, who lived four and a half hours away in California.

It may seem as though I hampered their relationship, but as a mother I refused to let a twenty-three-year-old man who had never kept his infants overnight or even during the day, drive four and a half hours on the freeway in a Volkswagen Beetle, with a two-year-old child and six-month-old infant in the back seat. Infants need to be changed and fed—not to mention the chaos that would ensue if either of them started to cry. Such a trip was an accident waiting to happen.

It wasn't until Chris was older and I made his grandparents meet me halfway that I let him visit. After they left, for days I would fall into depression, worrying about them.

After the divorce, at the insistence of my mother, Sally, I moved in with her for a year and a half. She loved my boys and spent many hours with them each day. My mother offered to watch Rett and Chris while I returned to college. I did attend classes for awhile, but I soon realized that having two vastly different, strong, independent women as caregivers was difficult and confusing for my children. We butted heads on many different levels, especially regarding the way my children should be disciplined.

I felt my only escape was to marry again, but like my first marriage, the second one was another huge mistake.

Rett was a stubborn, strong-willed and precocious child in need of a steady hand and strong yet loving discipline. He and my new husband didn't get along and soon the relationship between the two became unbearable.

When Rett was six years old, I decided to send him to live with his father in Texas. Although I'd sent my son away to save him, Rett thought I'd done it because I didn't love him.

I felt like a failure. My life was out of control and I desperately needed some peace. I remember sitting down with my husband shortly after we were married and trying to discuss my feelings. Not once did he take responsibility for any of the issues I brought to his attention. It was always somehow my fault.

Chris was two and a half years old when we first moved to my second husband's house. He was so frightened, in the middle of the night, he would quietly slip into our bedroom. A little tug on my nightgown would rouse me from sleep and I would let him crawl into bed next to me.

I can still remember his little body snuggled up against mine, the smell of his hair, the warmth of his skin.

Seconds later a voice would demand that I put him back in his room. I would carry Chris to his bed and tuck him in once again. I hated my husband for asking this of me, yet hated myself even more for obeying him. Why did I let those precious moments with my son slip past me? Why didn't I stand up for myself and what I thought was best?

I know now that I was fearful of being alone. Like most girls at that time, I was raised to believe that I needed a husband or male partner in order to survive. I did whatever I could to keep that lie in place, even if it meant going against what I knew in my heart was right.

My husband was raised by an alcoholic, abusive stepfather. He believed that intimidation was the best way to handle a problem. If that didn't work, he would physically make others bend to his will. Both of my sons were afraid of him and hated him because of his disciplinary tactics. I think they hated me too, for subjecting them to his abuse.

I tried my best to keep the boys away from him. The only gift that came from the marriage was my daughter, Kristin, conceived a year and a half after we were married, on the night I told my husband I wanted a divorce.

I had just returned from Christmas vacation in Hawaii with my dad, stepmom and her children; I'd left my boys in Reno with my mother, who lived only thirty minutes away from us.

I wished I'd told my husband by telephone that I wanted a divorce, but I felt it should be done in person. I was young, stupid and afraid of him.

I moved out immediately. A month later when he found out I was pregnant, he accused me of sleeping with someone else. This was an ugly accusation and completely untrue. In any serious relationship I'd ever had, marriage or otherwise, I had never been unfaithful.

After six months apart we reconciled and the boys and I moved back in with him. Kristin was born and then it went downhill from there. We remodeled a house and moved to Reno.

I remember one night in particular when we were lying in bed having a discussion. As soon as I injected my opinion—I may have even been flip about it—he was on top of me, one hand white knuckled at my throat, the other hand drawn back and balled into a fist ready to smash my face.

I remember thinking I was going to die. Who would take care of my babies? It was a sobering moment.

In the film *Sleeping With the Enemy* that appeared several years later, the man who played opposite Julia Roberts reminded me of my second husband. He not only looked like him; he also possessed the same type of charm with two distinct personalities.

As I watched Chris grow, I could see his gentle spirit touch those around him, yet his father and my second husband had left their mark. Whom could he trust? Certainly not the men in his life, nor his mother's ability to choose them. Fortunately, my younger brother, Peter, "Uncle Peter," was able to fill that place. The two were very close and Chris came to love him as the father he never really had.

Chris was athletic, intelligent and inquisitive, and he loved animals. I stood on the sidelines at each soccer and Little League game, and supported him through Cub Scouts and Boy Scouts. Although he had lots of friends and enjoyed school sports and other activities, even at a young age there was something deeper, wiser and older about him that set him apart from his peers.

When Kristin arrived four years later, I allowed Chris a longer leash and more freedom while I tended to his sister's infant needs.

My third husband was altogether different. Since he worked late and didn't arrive home until after midnight, our lifestyle changed considerably. We would spend late night "kitchen time" together while he ate his dinner. I would hold my sides laughing at our dumb jokes.

He was a calm port after a stormy sea. I felt safe with him because he was kind and loving and I knew he would never hurt me or my children.

The down side to the marriage was my husband's strong sex drive. He had to have his needs met every day or he would pout. With sex, life ran smoothly. Without sex, I lived with the consequences. It was an easy choice at the beginning. Finally there was some happiness in our home.

Chris got along famously with my new husband. It made me feel good to see a big grin light up my little boy's face when my husband walked through the door. If one of the kids needed me in the middle of the night, my new husband was there to support us and pitch in.

During this time, even though we had a bit of happiness, the shadow of my previous marriage still stalked us relentlessly. My daughter, Kristin was two years old when we divorced. The court ordered visitation two weekends a month. Next to burying my son, giving Kristin to her father for those mandatory weekends was one of the most difficult things I ever had to do. Kristin was terrified of her father.

When he showed up to take her, she would hang onto the wooden finials on the sofa, red-faced and screaming, begging me not to make her go.

I would have to peel my little girl's fingers off the knobs and carry her out to the driveway where I was forced to put her into his car.

Instantly when she saw her father, Kristin would become stoic and rigid. She would stare at me like I had betrayed her—and I had. I wanted to die rather than hurt my child, but I was afraid my ex-husband would kill me if I kept her from him. I was terrified of him.

All weekend I was a wreck, worrying about her. He would spank her if she cried for me, and throw her into her room. It upset my new husband and Chris, who hated this man even more than Kristin and I did.

On Sunday evening when Kristin would return, she wouldn't look at or speak to me for two days. I was in hell. This man still controlled our lives.

Summers were even worse. Once we moved out of state, Kristin was forced to visit for six weeks straight. It was traumatizing for her. In the beginning when we spoke by telephone she would start to cry and beg to come home. After these tearful conversations, he would punish her. My only recourse was to not speak with my child for the entire time she was with her father. Thank God my mom was there to intervene, check on Kristin and do the communicating for me.

Chris looked after his sister and protected her as best as he could; I could see the look in his eyes when Kristin's father would arrive. Had Chris been an adult, I think he may have killed him.

My older son, Rett, had little in common with Chris. They'd always fought with each other. Chris and Kristin, however, were kindred souls. From the very beginning they had a special bond. These two children knew and understood each other even without speaking. It was as if they were in their own secret universe.

I was keenly aware of something unusual about the two of them. I remember one summer at Glenbrook at Lake Tahoe—they were probably ages five and nine at the time—when both came to me with the same strange story at different times. They had been playing in the tree line near the beach, standing about thirty feet apart, when suddenly they looked at each other with their mouths open and a finger pointing in the direction of the tree line.

Both of them had the look of "Did you see that?" on their faces. They had witnessed what they described as dark shadow people running and hiding behind the trees. It unsettled me as I listened. I tried to briefly explain what they had seen without frightening them and then I changed the subject.

It wasn't until I had divorced my third husband several years later and we moved to Ketchum, Idaho in 1990 that their experiences became more prevalent. Both were aware of presences in each house we had moved into. Kristin would take little sticks, twigs, bright colored yarn and sparkles and make what she called fairy houses. She would then take the little houses into the woods and leave them there for the fairies. I thought it was cute, but I also honored her openness, curiosity and imagination. I made it a point to listen to their experiences without judgment. After all, I knew there was more to life than what I could actually see. I remember wishing that I would have had someone safe and open minded to confide in when I was a child.

In the meantime I had met a man who would eventually

become the father of my youngest daughter, Olivia. He was the person who introduced me to spirituality. As I learned from him I shared this new information with Chris and Kristin. Chris had become withdrawn since our move; he wanted nothing to do with the new man in my life. I couldn't blame him. He had already experienced so much instability and change, at this point he decided he wasn't going to open up emotionally for any more of my male choices. I understood.

Chris was fourteen and Kristin was ten when Olivia was born. Now a teenager, Chris was spending a great deal of time with his friends and a special young girl named Mandi. Mandi and her mother, Barbara became a refuge for Chris. He really cared about them and stepped in to the role of protector for Mandi.

Unfortunately, without full-time supervision, Chris had started drinking with friends and stopped participating at school. He became more defiant when I requested that he be home at certain times to participate in family gatherings.

I took him to counseling, but it didn't help. Repeatedly I gave him second chances to turn around his rapidly declining behavior and as a last resort I enrolled him in St. John's Military Academy in Delafield, Wisconsin.

My uncles had attended St. John's and it was suggested by family members that it could be the right place for Chris.

Soon after his enrollment, Chris begged me to come home. I was heartsick when I learned at a later time that while he was attending the Academy he had been abused by the students.

In his junior year, Chris transferred to a Catholic day

school in Reno and went to live with my mom. She tried to discipline him, but I think he usually charmed his way out of any predicament with her. Nonetheless, she came to really know and love my son.

In high school, Chris met Samantha. They dated for a few years and moved in together with a few other roommates. At that time Chris was partying and had no real motivation to work. Life had been a struggle for him and he carried a lot of pain and anger.

When Samantha decided to move out of state to live with her parents, she and Chris broke up. Shortly after, Samantha realized she was pregnant.

I knew the heartache and difficulty of raising a child at a young age and was not in favor of Samantha keeping the pregnancy. However, a good friend of Samantha's had recently given birth and after visiting her friend, Samantha decided to keep the baby.

I could not be more blessed to have such a darling grandson. Logan is truly remarkable.

At that point in Chris' life, my brother Peter suggested that Chris attend a spiritual rehabilitation program that he had attended. I spoke to Chris about this, apologizing to him about all the bad decisions I'd made in his life, and telling him how deeply sorry I was that he'd been so hurt.

"This is the last thing I can do for you, that may help rectify in some small way the wrongs I have inflicted on you," I told him. I made it clear, however, that the decision had to be his and not mine.

Chris agreed to go through the program and a month later he emerged a different person.

The change was phenomenal. He was poised, confident, ready and able to be a contributing part of society. My tears flowed freely at this second chance for my son, and the gift of reprieve from my grievous mistakes as a young mother.

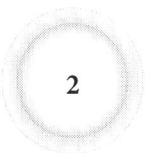

2

Shelly's Story

The Knowing

I do not consider myself a "religious" person. I was raised as a Christian Scientist, but only attended church a handful of times that I could remember. I attended a Catholic girl's boarding school, married a Mormon, an Atheist and a Baptist, dated a Jew, and had friends from all sects. Something was missing from each and I continued to search until I was introduced to Spirituality at the age of thirty.

At last, this was truth, my truth. I resonated with each new concept I learned, or maybe I should say that each spiritual principle or rule that was presented to me seemed to refresh my memory.

I wanted to know more; my appetite was voracious. I read all the books I could find or that were recommended to me on the subject of spirituality.

On the day my son, Christopher, was born I inhaled his scent, his presence, and his beauty. As I held him in my arms and love poured from my heart, I was swept up in the miracle of the moment.

I had always thought that if you didn't believe there was a God, you surely would change your mind the moment you held your newborn.

Love for Chris bloomed instantly. On that day something else happened. As I held my newborn in my arms for the first time, a terrible knowing swept through me.

I knew my son would die before I did.

This knowing was different from the inkling or feeling I would get from my intuition. It was an unerring *certainty* that shook me to my very core.

For twenty-five years I prayed for his safety. I prayed that my *knowing* was wrong and purposely pushed the thought from my mind. From time to time when it would rear its ugly head, I would say my affirmations and push it away.

Yet, as positive as I tried to remain, I still felt the need to prepare myself for the news that I was aware would inevitably come. Little did I know then that nothing can prepare a mother for a moment like that.

When I received the phone call from my brother, Peter on February 4, 2006 telling me that Chris had been killed in a motorcycle accident, my deepest sorrow and worst fear had come true.

I remember exhaling a long, stress-filled breath as I realized *it was finally over.* I had lived nearly every moment of the past twenty-five years knowing this call would come, and now my beautiful son was gone.

My heart was crushed. The only comfort I could find was the other *knowing* that he was finally home. He was finally safe.

"52"

In the mid 1990s I was living in Ketchum, Idaho. Chris was attending school in Wisconsin and he would visit on holidays. One day out of the blue Chris told me he knew how and when he was going to die. Caught completely off guard by his statement, I asked him to explain. He said he didn't want to worry me and that he would not disclose this information.

Worry me? Was he kidding? I had never revealed to him the knowing I'd had at his birth about his crossing over before me. I argued with him, to no avail. He wouldn't tell me.

Over the course of the next few years, I would ask him off and on for an answer, but he continued to be evasive until I cornered him one day in the kitchen. I was desperate. I told him I *had* to know.

He stared at me for a moment, weighing whether or not he should divulge the information and then he finally answered, "52, Mom. I'm going to die when I'm 52."

I asked him how he would die, but he flatly refused to tell me. He kept saying he didn't want to worry me.

It wasn't until a year or so after his accident that I remembered our strange conversation. He had told me "52," but that wasn't correct. He died when he was 25. Instantly I saw the numbers reverse themselves in my mind. My son had given me the correct digits, but he had purposely given them to me in the wrong order.

Coincidence? No, I don't believe so. I really think he *did* know when he was going to cross over and was determined to protect me, regardless of how much I pressured him for an answer.

I will never know how he knew when he was going to die and he never disclosed to me the way in which it would occur. One thing I do know is that Chris was aware of how adamantly opposed I was to his owning a motorcycle. He and a friend had each purchased a motorcycle a few weeks before his accident, but Chris didn't tell anyone in his family.

Premonition

In June of 2005, my mother, Sally, Chris' grandmother, phoned to suggest we all take a trip to Disneyland. She thought the best time would be during the fall when the youngest grandchildren had their three-week break from year-round school.

My mom loved to bring family together. It meant so much to her, often she would make plans a year ahead if possible. We all grumbled when she pressed us for advance calendar dates because most of us had no idea what we would be doing a year from then.

On this occasion, even though October was only four months away, I got snippy with her when she pressed me for an answer. "Geez, Mom, why do you have to know right now? This is the third time you've called in two days!"

"Because I have to make the reservations," she countered. "Peter's going to drive me down there. Stephen and Katie [Stephen's wife] and the kids are going." She told me that Chris and Logan, who now lived in Dallas, would also be flying in.

"Off-hand I can't tell you the exact dates Olivia and I can go. I still have to check her school calendar." I tried not to sound irritated but I couldn't help adding, "Why do you have to make this such a big deal?"

The phone went silent for a moment and then my mom answered resolutely, "Because this may be the last trip we all take together. One of us might not be here next year."

I brushed off her comment and we said goodbye.

Olivia and I were able to join the rest of the family at Disneyland after all, and we had a great time. I have many photos of all of us laughing and having fun together.

We also spent a few days at Laguna Beach visiting my aunt and uncle. On the last day of the trip we met a group of cousins and had lunch at the Balboa Bay Club in Newport Beach.

While the younger ones played in the sand, Olivia and Chris had a chance to spend time together. Olivia loved her brother and the separation was difficult for both of them. Their reunions were always too brief.

When it was time to leave, a few of us were waiting for our cars at the valet. Chris and Logan's vehicle had already been delivered and they were about to drive away.

My brother, Stephen, was still busy rounding up his children. Suddenly he looked over at Chris' vehicle and said, "I'd better go and say goodbye to Chris. I don't know when I'll see him again."

That was the last time my brother and most of my family saw my son. Four months later he was gone. Sometimes, it's not until we are able to look back on life's particular situations that we see how much we are guided by Spirit.

And He Shall Prepare The Way

In December of 2005 I met a man online at a well known dating site. Three months earlier, his college age daughter had been tragically killed in a car accident. What attracted me to his profile was his spiritual approach to life and the way he had accepted this tragedy. Clearly it was an event that had added even greater strength to the spiritual fiber of his life.

I emailed him and we started to discuss our spiritual beliefs, first online and then by phone. We talked about many things, including his daughter's passing and the aftermath.

My heart went out to him because I could feel the pain of his loss—and yet I admired his strength and courage, his unwavering belief that everything was really in divine order, after all.

I had never lost someone with whom I was close. It had been a long time since I'd dwelled on the "what if" scenario of losing a child. Somehow through the years I'd pushed that thought aside, but now once again, my conversation with this man caused me to wonder how I would respond if one of my children were killed.

As I listened to his account of the miraculous things that had happened since his daughter's crossing, I was amazed by what he was telling me. He said she continued to let her father know that she was still there with him.

"In January I plan to go to India to spread her ashes in an ashram," he said. "My daughter's birthday is February 3, only a short time away."

I didn't realize at the time that these discussions had tapped into that deep inner knowing that I'd always had about my son—a *knowing* that was supposed to serve as a way of preparing me in advance.

It felt good to share these feelings with someone who had actually been through such an experience.

A little more than a month later I received the phone call from Peter that Chris had been killed in an accident.

I had been 90% accurate about the way I would handle the loss of a child, but I didn't come anywhere close to comprehending the level of pain that enveloped every part of my being.

On the day my son died, my old life stopped and a new

one began. Regardless of any so-called preparation, without a doubt, it was the worst day of my life.

Was it merely a coincidence that I had recently met someone who had just lost a child? That I had spent time discussing the experience and how I would handle it, just before it happened to me?

No, it was no coincidence. Spirit was guiding and preparing me for my son's crossing. God works in mysterious and wonderful ways. *Thank you, God. Thank you, Spirit.*

The least I could do now was to be open to the possibility of contact with my son. I had taught him about life after death. I now had someone with whom to communicate.

Rationally, I knew there was little time to dwell in a state of misery and sadness. I was a mother with two daughters who needed my support. Chris' little boy, Logan, my grandson, also needed me. I tried to imagine what he was going through.

Physically, I had no control. My body was going to grieve, regardless of how spiritual and open-minded I was. Yes, I cried and wailed, but mostly in private.

I was the glue that held the family together. They would look to me for strength and guidance while they fell apart. My youngest daughter, Olivia, told me later that she didn't think I was sad about Chris' dying since she didn't really see me cry when I heard the news.

Olivia didn't realize that I didn't break down in front of her because I had no one to pick me up. I refused to put that responsibility on an eleven-year-old child.

Directly following Chris' accident, my aunt and uncle graciously invited members of the family to use their home in Laguna Beach, California as a base while we went about the painful task of taking care of necessary details.

By the time we arrived, my cousin and her husband were already there to lend support. Two years earlier their son, a sixteen-year-old, had been killed in a car accident. Through the family grapevine, I learned that my cousin had said, "At least someone else knows how I feel."

I do, indeed, know how she feels. It is more than devastating to experience the loss of a child. Both she and her husband have a strong faith in God and attend church regularly. I know how this commitment has helped them cope with their loss.

Although I did not attend church, regardless of our differing beliefs, our God was the same and both of us knew the power of that bond.

It wasn't until I began to awaken to the miracles happening around me on almost a daily basis that I began to understand the bigger picture. Eventually I came to realize that I wasn't "just imagining" these miracles. Anything really was possible!

Even before Chris had crossed over, I strongly believed a person could be proactive in communicating with a child or loved one after they departed.

I knew the typical ways that connections were made. They came as dreams that were so vivid you would swear they were real. You may smell the scent of your mother's favorite perfume or Grandpa's cigar. You may feel a touch or a presence around you. The lights may blink, or just as you're thinking of that person, a song will be played on the radio that reminds you of them.

You may see their name written in an unusual place just

after the thought of them pops into your mind. You may even hear their voice or see a vision of them.

People have also had unusual experiences with animals or birds. Sometimes you may even get validation of an experience through a friend or medium.

On several occasions I had attempted to discuss this belief with my cousins, but invariably the conversation was cut short. After awhile I realized they were not ready for this information and Spirit was deliberately stopping me.

I continue to be hopeful that one day they will be open to consider this opportunity. People don't realize how much they miss if they are unfamiliar with after-death communication[1] (ADC) and the comfort these remarkable experiences can bring to those who have suffered a loss.

The weekend of Chris' crossing, my younger brother, Peter, took charge as usual. His pain was palatable, yet he remained stoic and refused to break, at least not in front of any of us. He had spent a lot of time with Chris throughout his life and as I mentioned previously, from an early age he had served as my son's father figure.

Peter, my older brother and a niece stayed at the nearby Inn at Laguna Beach. This was the same hotel where we had reserved rooms four months earlier, when the entire family, including Chris and Logan, had visited Disneyland.

---

[1] "**After Death Communication (ADC)** is a spiritual experience, which occurs when you are contacted *directly* and *spontaneously* by a deceased family member or friend, *without* the use of psychics, mediums, rituals, or devices of any kind. It's estimated that 50-100 million Americans - 20-40% of the population of the United States - have had one or more ADC experiences. Therefore, ADCs provide convincing new evidence for life after death." Bill and Judy Guggenheim, authors of *Hello From Heaven!*, and their website www.after-death.com.

Uncle Peter's Story

Father's Day In Cancun

Kristin, Chris and Uncle Peter

In June 2005 I was contemplating moving to Mexico from Dallas. For three weeks, I visited various towns and cities from northern Mexico to Mexico City and finally ended the journey in Cancun. Chris and his sister, Kristin joined me in Cancun for the last week. Kristin had finished her second year at Southern Methodist University and Chris was out of school for a few weeks, so I thought it would be fun for them to come down to the beach and spend time together.

Chris was a fun travel companion and a delight to have on a trip. He was up for any new adventure and always had a smile on his face. We found ourselves in Cancun for Chris' twenty-fifth birthday as well as Fathers' Day.

Kristin and Chris had a unique dynamic. Chris had the ability to get Kristin to try new and different things and really make her laugh. Watching them interact was a treat. It was obvious they had a special relationship and were probably the closest of friends.

While we were in Mexico, we shopped for an apartment. We looked at many of the modern residential buildings on the coast, directly north of the American hotels. One of the high rise apartments had five bedrooms and a view of the ocean, with a great beach. It was certainly a possibility until I found out it had no fire system. The real estate agent assured me there were no fires in Cancun, which was probably why the builders hadn't thought to include one.

Chris and Kristin felt the apartment was okay, but they weren't sure that Mexico was the place to buy. Without considering the matter further, we headed down the coast for dinner.

Since it was Father's Day, Chris suggested sushi at a Japanese restaurant located in a high-end hotel. He loved all types of food and was a good sport about trying new dishes. Frankly, I was so tired of Mexican food, sushi sounded great.

At dinner we wished Chris a Happy Father's Day and as we did so, a shadow passed over his face. His jovial mood changed to one of pensiveness and introspection.

"Today is Fathers' Day and my dad wouldn't think of calling me," he said, his face registering his sadness. "Nor do I feel enough of a connection to call him."

The comment greatly moved me and I didn't know how to respond. I felt his pain and could see his disappointment.

Thankfully, Kristin chimed in and said to me, "You were the only real father either of us ever had, Uncle Peter."

Chris nodded in agreement. "That's true, Uncle Peter. I could always count on you."

I smiled and replied, "And I will always be there for you. It is really my great joy that I can spend time with you both. By the way, our next adventure together is Istanbul!"

At that point we launched into a serious discussion of what was important in life and the ones we could count on to be there for us. I mentioned to Chris and Kristin that we could depend on very few people when we needed them. Unfortunately, the fathers in our lives were not men whom one could ever count on for much. They would show up for a graduation, maybe make a small gesture at birthday time, and possibly call a few times a year with the usual pleasantries. You certainly would not bet your life or your child's life on them. We had accepted them for who they were and moved past our disappointment.

We all agreed that my mother, Sally, or Piggy, as the grandchildren called her, was there for us with absolute unconditional love. We felt we could tell her anything and she would love us no matter what. I told Chris that he needed to care for me when I was old and make the tough decisions about the end of my life. He was really upset and didn't want to think of my death.

"You are the tough one, Chris," I said. "I can only count on you. You have to do it because you actually care about me." He smiled and was reassured that I really needed him.

Suddenly Chris started talking about Logan, his four-and-a-half year old son. His eyes began to tear. "I love Logan so much," he said with a broad smile. "If anything happens to me, would you take care of him?" Without waiting for a response, he kept talking, since both of us knew it was a rhetorical question. "Promise me three things. First, make sure he can spend time with Piggy in Reno. Second, make sure he is well educated. Third, let him see my dad's side of the family once he's big enough to run away from them if he should need to."

It was obvious he had been thinking about Logan's future, that it was not just a casual comment. I could tell he was recalling the time he had visited his dad's family over Christmas as a seven year old. Unsupervised, he'd accidentally caught his gloved hand in a drill. The drill had instantly snapped his index finger between his hand and first knuckle. Hysterical, he had called both his mother and grandmother, but regardless of their insistence to the adults in charge that Chris needed medical assistance, neither his dad nor his grandparents felt it was necessary.

Ten days later when they returned him to my sister, Shelly, she took one look at Chris' hand and rushed him to the hospital. The doctor on call nearly accused her of child abuse. They had to re-break and then re-set Chris' index finger to prevent it from interfering with his ability to properly use his thumb and forefinger later on.

Clearly, Chris wanted to keep Logan from suffering a similar trauma. His question was more a reassurance that I would care for Logan's well-being no matter what. I readily agreed.

We stayed in Mexico for a few more days while the kids played at the beach. The three of us were so happy we could spend such quality time together.

Kristin left for Texas a few days later and Chris and I spent an extra week in Cozumel and Playa del Carmen before returning to Dallas.

Little did we know that this would be our last big trip and adventure together. Seven months later, Chris was gone.

The conversation during our Mexican trip took on even greater significance after his death. It was as if Chris somehow knew his life was about to end and our lives were to change forever.

Hurricane Katrina hit Cancun in August and destroyed the hotel we'd stayed in, the Japanese restaurant where we had dinner and the apartment we'd considered buying.

Chris and Kristin saved me from making a bad investment in Mexico. We decided that Reno, where the family lived, would be a much better place to be and in August, 2005 I decided to sell my Dallas home and move there.

Room 420

It was a gorgeous morning in Dallas that first Saturday in February 2006. A bright blue sky and crisp weather were a welcome contrast to the heat that would follow in only a few weeks. I was heading to my brother's house to watch a Stars hockey game on TV when the silence was broken by the ring of my cell phone.

It was the Dallas police department. The officer asked if I knew a Christopher Arrington. When I said yes, he was my nephew, the officer explained that he needed to speak with me and asked me to pull over if I were driving. I insisted we speak in person and met the police at my house.

Chris had moved from Dallas to Hollywood a couple

months ago, shortly after several members of the family, including Shelly, Olivia, Chris and Logan, had traveled to California for a memorable Disneyland adventure.

The news of Chris' death was shattering. Somehow I remained composed while in a state of disbelief and at a complete loss about what to do next.

I had been the first to be told the news, so my first call was to my sister, Shelly. Within hours I was on a plane to my aunt and uncle's house in Laguna Beach. The only hotel I was familiar with was the Inn at Laguna where we had stayed four months earlier. I stood at the empty reception desk, exhausted and numb, and waited for the clerk. It was 11PM. Nineteen hours had passed since the Dallas police had delivered the news of Chris' death.

A woman appeared and quickly checked me in with a pleasant "Welcome back."

Noting that I was tired and disoriented, she told me she'd given me a room just off the elevator on the fourth floor. I didn't respond to her or to her question of whether my visit was for business or pleasure. I just headed for the elevator.

"Fourth floor," she called out again.

As the clerk had said, the room was just to the right as I exited the elevator. Room 420.

Upon opening the door, I was instantly aware that she had given me the exact room I had shared with Chris and his son, Logan, in October.

What kind of trick was this? Memories of that wonderful trip assaulted me with such force I finally broke down and cried. It was as if I'd seen a ghost. Within minutes I returned to the front desk, visibly upset and shaken, and demanded a different room. The clerk complied without any questions.

As I look back on that experience I realize its significance. It was Chris' way of letting me know he was still here with me.

A few weeks later I had a sleep-state ADC[2], an After-Death Communication. It was so clear and real. I was standing in the viewing room at the coroner's office. The room was white and Chris was lying on the gurney draped with a white sheet pulled up to his chest. He looked at peace as if he were just sleeping.

I said to myself, "What a pity. It's so sad."

Suddenly, as if he had heard me, Chris' head snapped to the left and he looked right at me and said, "You're next."

Five years later I would like to report that I am still present and accounted for, but I would also like to note that no one in our immediate family has crossed over since then.

---

[2] **"Sleep-state ADCs** feel like actual face-to-face visits with deceased loved ones. They are much more orderly, colorful, vivid, and memorable than most dreams." *Hello From Heaven!* by Bill and Judy Guggenheim, copyright 1995.

Kristin's Story

Three Friends

On the weekend of February 4, 2006 I was at home working on a project for one of my college classes. In September I had transferred from Southern Methodist University in Texas to Santa Clara University in California. I lived about ten minutes from the campus, so I often worked at home on the weekends instead of driving to the university library. On that morning, however, I felt a strange nudge to do my homework at school. I've learned not to argue with my intuition so I packed my books and headed to the library.

After a few hours of working on my papers, I received a voicemail from my mom saying that I needed to call her back immediately and that I needed to be sitting down when I called. I could tell by the tone of her voice that something serious had happened.

Since my little sister, Olivia, lives with my mom the first thoughts that went through my mind were, "Something has happened to Olivia!"

I hurried out of the library and placed a call to my mother. When she answered, all I can remember her saying was, "Kristin, Chris is dead. He was killed last night. He died in a motorcycle accident."

I can still remember the wave of shock, disbelief and utter horror that washed through me when I heard those words. My brother, Chris was the single most important person in my life. *He was my life.*

Chris was my best friend, my soul mate and someone I could not live without. I was overcome by such indescribable, unyielding pain, I felt time and space screech to a halt. My legs crumbled beneath me as I fell to the floor. I remember screaming between sobs in a desperate attempt to relieve the overwhelming pain in my body and heart.

My mom was still on the phone and I remember her begging me to go to the counselor's office. "Don't drive home!" she pleaded.

I told her I wouldn't, but the moment I hung up I ran straight to the parking garage to get my car.

I had parked on the top or third level so I took the elevator to the third floor. Incoherent and completely inconsolable, I waited for what felt like eons for the elevator to reach the top floor. When the doors opened, three women stood before me. Blinking back my tears I realized they weren't just any three women; they were the only three friends I had met so far at my new school. When they saw the condition I was in, they scooped me up, took me to the counseling center, and along with the Jesuit priests, spent the rest of the day praying with me and consoling me.

On a campus of eighty-seven hundred students, what are the chances of my only three friends at school appearing in front of me at the worst moment of my life? I'd guess a million to one. In my heart I know that my brother nudged me to head to school that day to do my homework. In my heart I know it was Chris who had positioned the only three women who could help me, between me and my car.

If I had been home alone when I had received the news of his death, or if I had tried to drive in such an emotional state, I'm not sure I would be here today.

Thank you, Chris, for your continued love and guidance. I am so blessed to still be connected to you.

5

Pam's Story

Reality TV

One night in May of 2001 I had the feeling that something terrible was going to happen to my dear friend, Susie. I knew I couldn't call her and mention it, so I shook it off and went to bed. Early the next morning the phone rang. My heart stood still as the caller delivered the terrible news. Susie's son, Matt, had been killed in a car accident the previous evening, one week before his 19th birthday. I had lived near Susie and her husband, and had watched Matt grow up. I was sick with grief and horrified by what I knew Susie and her husband, Steve must be going through. The caller told me that the services would be held in a week or so and they would keep me posted.

All morning as I packed for a trip, a bird kept pecking at the window. My grandmother had always believed that this was a sign that foretold a death. A week later I joined Susie and Steve in Seattle to say goodbye to their son, Matt. If there was a question of who Matt had touched and the friends he'd helped during his short life, it was surely answered at the moving memorial that his friends had arranged. There must have been more than a thousand people in attendance. Although Susie was a pillar of strength, Steve and I fell apart.

Shortly after the funeral, I moved to a new house. The

following year in February 2002, I was awakened in the middle of the night by the sound of trumpets and Bob Costa's voice. I hurried upstairs to find the TV blasting away with the Olympics.

That's odd, I thought. *Who turned on the TV?* I had the distinct impression that I wasn't alone in the room, yet I wasn't frightened. I could simply feel that someone was there with me.

Over the next few weeks, the same thing continued to happen. The TV would just pop on in the middle of the night and when I went upstairs to turn it off, I felt I wasn't alone.

I called the cable company and they sent out someone to check the connections to the TV. Everything was normal. They had no explanation for it. The more I thought about it, the more I felt that someone was trying to connect with me. *Who could that be?*

Then it dawned on me that it was Matt. I had a reading with a well known psychic to confirm my suspicions. She validated my feelings and I shared all of this with Susie, Matt's mother. Susie was totally convinced of the connection.

Within a year or so I lost my darling miniature horse, Silver, who died in my arms. I was beside myself with grief. He had been such a large part of my life.

Later that night after consoling myself with a few glasses of wine, I said out loud, "Matt, if you are here, you have to tell me that Silver is with you and that he's okay!"

A little while later, I turned off the TV. As I headed across the living room towards the staircase and my bedroom downstairs, the TV popped back on! It startled me for a moment and then I remembered my earlier plea to Matt for help.

I had received confirmation that Silver had arrived safely on The Other Side!

"Thank you," I cried out loud. "Thank you!" My feelings of my connection to Matt were confirmed in my heart.

During the following year, I moved once again and my TV continued to pop on by itself every few weeks. When it did, I would pick up the phone and call Susie, Matt's mother. I always felt it was Matt's way of encouraging Susie and me to stay in touch.

Then late one night on February 3, 2006, I was awakened once again by the TV popping on. Irritated by the sudden arousal from a sound sleep, I muttered to myself, *What now?*

As I trudged upstairs a feeling of complete dread came over me.

When I reached the top of the staircase I said out loud, "This is not good." I paused for a moment, then turned off the TV. In my gut I knew something terrible had happened. I knew this wasn't a reminder to call Susie and chat the next day.

As bad as I felt, I also knew there was nothing I could do. Whatever was going on would reveal itself in good time.

The next morning when I was upstairs in the kitchen and thinking about what had happened in the middle of the night, the phone rang.

It was my friend, Shelly. She told me that her son, Chris, had been killed last night in a motorcycle accident. I was shocked and stunned. How do you even start to console a mother who has just lost her child? I mentioned to her what had happened with the TV. Suddenly the message became clear. Matt had tried to warn me. All I could do was let Shelly know that someone very special was with her son, Chris, helping him on his journey to The Other Side. It was my friend, Matt.

Mandi's Story

Friends Forever

When you are young and meet someone for the first time, you have no way of knowing how important that person will be, or the impact he will have on your life. Many people may never experience the true friendship and love that I was fortunate enough to share with Chris.

The first time I saw Chris I was eleven years old and living in Hailey, Idaho. I had enrolled in a modeling class to learn how to walk, talk, and present myself properly. Chris' mom taught the class in her home. That day I was sitting at the dining room table, deep in thought, desperately trying to remember the difference between the salad and dessert fork.

Suddenly the silence was broken by giggling. I glanced up and saw Chris and his friend leaning over the balcony, spying on us. I was mortified to have been caught in such an awkward moment. Later that day, I thought back on the incident and wished I had been able to toss off some smart remark to put him in his place.

About a year later, at the beginning of seventh grade, as I was passing through the hallway with my friends, I noticed a guy walking towards us. As he approached, I realized it was Chris, the same guy who had laughed at me the year before when I was caught in the salad-dessert fork dilemma at his mom's house. Chris recognized me and smiled as he walked by. I had an immediate crush.

We crossed paths a few more times before Chris cornered me by my locker. I knew he was standing directly behind me, but I pretended not to notice. I shut my locker and turned around.

"Are you watching me?" he asked, a huge smile on his face.

I was nearly struck mute but managed, "No. Are you watching me?"

He laughed at my comeback, then turned and headed towards his next class. It was only a few weeks later that Chris asked me to be his girlfriend. Of course I said yes! There was something about this guy that made everyone, including me, want to be near him.

Chris was funny, silly, sweet, and everything a girl would want for their first real boyfriend. Even though I was very young, I was instantly in love with him. I knew he loved me too and would always be there to protect me. I remember thinking that we would be together forever.

Later that year, Chris got into some trouble at home. When I saw him at school he had some bad news for me. He was being sent to St. John's Military Academy in Wisconsin in less than a week. My whole world came crashing down. We spent as much time together as we could. We professed our love and promised to remain true.

We wrote to each other constantly, sometimes three or four letters a week. I nagged my mother to drive to the post office every day to check for a letter from Chris.

We wrote about everything, including how much we loved and missed each other, and especially how much he *hated* military school.

Our young, long distance love relationship endured until the summer before my freshman year of high school when we decided it was too difficult to remain exclusive. We stayed in constant contact and when we talked it felt like nothing had changed.

The following year, Chris left military school to live with his grandmother in Reno and attend Bishop Manogue Catholic high school. He was much happier there than he'd been in military school. He still missed me, but was glad to leave the 4AM military marches behind.

Later that year Chris met me, my mom and some friends in Las Vegas. We had a great week together. It was as if nothing had changed between us, despite the fact that we were four years older. He even rented a limo to cruise the Strip and he presented me with a dozen roses. He always knew how to make me feel special.

Sadly, once again, we heard ourselves saying goodbye, a recurring event in our relationship. It always felt like there was never enough time.

A year later I was living in San Francisco attending a high school program at the Art Academy. Chris asked me if I would fly to Reno and spend the Fourth of July with him in Tahoe. The first day we went to Warp Tour where we saw Eminem and many other bands. Later, we went to Chris' cabin where Chris, his friends and I watched the fireworks over Lake Tahoe. It was absolutely the best and my most memorable Fourth of July ever!

At the end of my junior year at Wood River High School in Hailey, Idaho, I called Chris and jokingly asked if he wanted to take me to the senior prom. He called the next day and said he'd booked a flight so I'd better find a dress. I was stunned!

He arrived a few weeks later with his tux in hand. We had a great night and everyone was really excited to see Chris again. I think they were surprised to see that Chris and I were still close after all those years.

After graduating from high school I moved back to California where I got involved in a horrible relationship. Something was wrong; I felt like I was losing my identity.

Chris would always check in with me to see how things were going. My boyfriend hated the fact that Chris and I were so close and tried to prevent me from speaking with him.

Chris also had a lot going on in his life. On November 2, 2000, he became a daddy when Logan Parker Arrington was born. Chris was a very proud daddy and always loved to call me to tell me about his son. I was very happy for him and so proud of him for being such a great dad to Logan.

The next few years passed rather quickly and by 2002, I was living in San Diego and struggling with a drug addiction. I had my own apartment but no job. Partying consumed my days and nights. My mom was incredibly worried about me and the only person she could really talk to about me was Chris.

I didn't know until later that Chris talked with my mom every week. He told her he would come to California to see me.

Chris thought that with his help I might be able to get clean. During his visit, he tried to convince me to move to Dallas where he was living.

I told him I'd think about it, but I knew in my heart that it wasn't his responsibility to help me come clean. If I wanted to drop the drug habit, I had to do this myself.

He was really disappointed. I think he always felt it was his job to take care of me. Broke and with no place to live, I decided to head for my mom's house in Idaho. Chris wired me a couple hundred dollars so I could rent a car to drive home.

After a few months I was clean. Chris was very excited for me and called constantly. He even sent me flowers to congratulate me. He also urged me to go back to school. He knew it was my dream to go to Art School. At the time he was attending The Art Institute of Dallas, pursuing a degree in video production.

Chris really wanted me to enroll at the Art Institute, but as luck would have it, I met a guy named Aric. He had a lot going for himself and had never been into drugs. Our relationship progressed quickly and we moved in together.

Chris was apprehensive at first, but quickly realized that Aric was different from the losers I'd dated in the past. He was happy for me and liked the fact that Aric treated me well. Chris and I had always had the understanding that if we couldn't be together, at least we wanted each other to be happy and healthy. Finally, after a long and rough road, I had found both.

Can You Hear Me Now?

At the end of January 2006 I got a text message from Chris, telling me how much he loved me and that he only wanted the best for me. He stated that he was happy for me and pleased to know that I was safe and happy. He told me that I was one of the most important persons in his life and he cherished all that we had been through together.

He also wrote that he would always be there for me—that no matter what—he would love me unconditionally. As I read his message, tears came to my eyes. I texted him back and told him I felt the same way, and that I loved him very much. I told him to call me in the next few days to catch up. He said he would.

I remember thinking the following day that the text message was rather unusual. Chris was always extremely affectionate towards me and bold when it came to expressing his feelings. Somehow this message seemed different.

The following week, Chris and I played phone tag. I was working a lot and he had just moved to Los Angeles with two friends, leaving Logan in Dallas with his mother. Although we kept missing each other's calls, I told myself that eventually we would catch up with each other.

Saturday morning my phone rang off the hook. My cell showed (000)-000-0000. Every time I would answer the call, it seemed like someone was on the other end talking very softly. There was static so I couldn't hear what they were saying. I would say, "Hello, hello," and try to listen to what was being said.

At the time I thought it might be a telemarketer, yet I thought it was weird that a telemarketer would be calling on the weekend nonstop and at all hours of the day.

I even received a call from the number at 3:30AM on Sunday. I was getting extremely frustrated and started to have the feeling that someone might be stalking me.

That weekend I was awakened in the middle of the night by a bright light in the bedroom. I got up, checked the hallway and went to the window to search outside. Everything was dark.

It seemed that this light was its own source. I didn't think much of it until a few weeks later when my mom mentioned something about a light in her room the weekend of Chris' accident. We both started to cry. It had to have been Chris trying to tell us something that had happened to him.

On Monday morning, February 6, I awoke and as usual, dressed and headed out to work. A little after noon, just as I was leaving a client's house, my cell phone rang.

It was Chris' number. I was excited! We would finally be able to catch up with each other. I remember answering the phone by saying, "Hey you!" and was surprised to hear Chris' mom on the other end. She asked me what I was doing and I told her I was working.

"Call me when you get home," she said. "I need to talk to you."

"I'll call you in a few hours," I promised. I could tell by the tone of Shelly's voice that something wasn't right.

What was going on? Maybe Chris had had a breakdown or something. I even thought maybe he was going to rehab, although I knew he wasn't on drugs. I couldn't figure out why she would be calling me from Chris' cell phone.

That evening I told Aric about the call from Chris' mom. He tried to reassure me that it was probably nothing too serious and I really wanted to believe him.

I dialed Shelly's number and as soon as I heard her voice I felt sick again. She told me that Chris had been killed in a motorcycle accident on Friday night.

What had she just said? I could scarcely remember. *What—?*

I couldn't speak.

"Are you okay, Mandi?" I heard her ask somewhere in the recesses of my mind. "Will someone be with you for the rest of the day?" she was asking.

I remember putting down the phone and starting to scream and cry hysterically. I ran into the bathroom and lunged toward the shower door. Aric rushed in after me and grabbed me. He held me and tried to calm me down.

A few minutes later my mom showed up. She was also hysterical. Chris had always been there for her and she thought of him like a son. I have had a lot of death in my life, but never had I experienced such pain as when I found out about Chris. It was unbearable.

The following week I was a complete wreck. I couldn't eat or sleep and was unable to go to work.

Several days later, Chris' text message came to mind. Pulling out my phone, I reread it. It was as if somehow he knew he was crossing over and had sent a last goodbye.

Shelly called me at the end of the week to ask how I was doing.

"Mandi," she said hesitantly," has anything unusual happened?"

I thought for a moment. "No, not really." Then I added, "Well, sort of."

I told her about the weird calls from the (000)-000-000 number that had shown up on my cell phone the weekend of Chris' accident. She got very excited and told me it was Chris trying to call me.

I really didn't believe in all that stuff, but after we hung up I began to wonder if it was possible. Was Chris' spirit calling me, trying to tell me that something had happened to him? At the time I received those calls, I hadn't heard the news of his death.

So many people in my life had died, and their passing had left me with the feeling of profound sadness and loss. I'd never considered any other possibility than death being THE END. Chris was the one friend who I knew would always be there for me.

The thought of his absence and finality of the situation was overwhelming. Yet that text message and those phone calls got me thinking. What if…*what if there was more to death than just THE END?*

Once I was able to leave my house without melting down, I went to the library and checked out as many books as I could about death and life after death.

That's when I discovered *Talking to Heaven*, by James Van Praagh, a book that changed my life. The author is a psychic medium and the book is about his experiences with people who have passed and their ability to communicate with their loved ones. This book made me realize that Chris and everyone else I had lost in my life were still very present. The book completely changed my understanding of death.

This revelation led me to contact my phone company to inquire about the person with the strange number who was calling me the weekend Chris was killed. My phone company told me there was no record at all of those incoming calls and there is no number (000) 000-0000.

Needless to say, I was both shocked and excited. I knew then that it had been Chris. He was trying to let me know what had happened to him. I felt so blessed knowing he was still around and trying to communicate with me.

Barbara's Story

Little Light Of Mine

My name is Barbara Patterson and I feel so honored to share my experiences about Chris since his crossing. It makes me smile just thinking of all my wonderful visits from him, and then I shed tears because I miss him so much.

I truly believe that certain people come into my life for a reason. I know that Chris is one of those persons. He came into my life not just for one reason, but for many. The first was to win the heart of my daughter, Mandi Lane. Chris was Mandi's first love. At the time I was a single mom raising Mandi alone.

When Chris was still very young, he won my trust and also my heart. He would just give me a look with his big puppy dog eyes and he had me. He also used his great half-grin, half-smile to win me over. He taught me to trust in Mandi and to have patience during her growing years when she was experimenting with things I did not approve of.

When I would worry and spend sleepless nights, Chris would phone to reassure me that Mandi would be okay. We would spend thirty or forty minutes visiting on the phone, talking about Mandi, and anything and everything that he was doing at the time. I loved those calls so much. He made me laugh and smile when I really needed to.

Since Chris' passing, I have come to love and enjoy those

visits that have now taken a different form.

The reason I am so open to "life after death" experiences is a book I read many years ago when I lost my girlfriend, Marilyn. It was such a painful loss that the book, *Talking to Heaven*, by James Van Praagh, was recommended to me to help me get through that experience. I learned to keep my mind open to the signs of loved ones in my everyday life after they had passed over. They really do have the power to stay in touch.

Chris's spirit was the strongest one ever to make contact with both Mandi and me.

On the weekend of February 4, I was awakened by a very bright light on the wall beside my bed. It seemed to radiate a lot of energy, more than the usual reflection of lights from outside.

I got out of bed to see where the strange light was coming from, but everything was dark outside. No car or street lights, nothing.

Days later, I learned of Chris' accident and of his passing. When sharing my story with Mandi, I learned that she had had a similar experience that night. We both cried and whispered Chris' name, knowing he had visited us.

8

Shelly's Story

Manifestation

Just before we left to visit the accident site, my aunt picked a glorious bouquet of calla lilies from her garden and tied it with a ribbon. I placed the flowers in the crook of the damaged chain link fence and stood for a moment in silence as the tails of the ribbon danced in the breeze. It was strange to see these flowers so out of place, but stranger still to be staring at the spot where my son had drawn his last breath. I read a few prayers and then we quietly returned to our vehicles for the drive to the Ventura County Coroner's office.

My two brothers, Bill and Peter, my niece and two daughters, Olivia and Kristin, waited while I went in to see my son. Stoically I walked down the hallway and pushed open the swinging door to the small room.

Through the glass windows on the other side of a double door I caught a glimpse of my son's body. It felt as if someone had suddenly punched me in the chest...hard. I staggered, gasped and clutched my heart against the blow, the scene, the reality that had not yet had a chance to solidify in my mind.

A single errant tear slid down my cheek as I willed myself not to break down.

How did we end up here? Like this...and why? What was the purpose of this seemingly senseless loss of life?

He lay on a gurney covered in pristine white sheets that were tucked up to his chin. They had already performed the autopsy. Having watched numerous medical shows on television, I knew what lay beneath those pristine sheets, yet I took in every inch of the scene before me. Mentally I touched him with my hands and ran my fingers through his hair. I stroked his brow, kissed his cheek and held him.

A life review of memories flashed through my mind: love, joy, pain, sorrow, frustration and regret. The last burned hottest and at moments still does. I had held him when he entered this world and above all I wished I could have held him when he left.

As I stood there feeling every bit sorry for myself and the decisions that may have landed both of us in this position, I became aware of more than just me. Something profound was happening and momentarily it sucked me out of my misery.

I was experiencing a shift in thought or energy, which one I couldn't be sure. I felt as if the scientist in me had stepped out of the mother's body. Suddenly I was acutely aware of the room, the air, the temperature, the sound or lack of it, and the lighting. It was surreal. I didn't know what was happening. What I did know was that my son was not in that body lying before me...*and he was not dead.*

The experience was profoundly life altering on many levels: first, as a mother who would never again physically hold her child; second, as a grandmother who grieved for the little boy he left behind; and third and most important, as a non-physical Higher or Inner Self that was imparting to me with absolute clarity that there are two distinct and separate parts to a human being: the physical and spiritual.

This was exactly what I had experienced at the age of eight, standing in the middle of my driveway. "God," I had asked then, "tell me why I am here." Now, at last, I realized I already held the answer to my question deep within. At eight years old, it was not time yet to be revealed.

I knew I was viewing Chris' shell and he was "not at home."

I felt physically frozen, yet everywhere at once. I realized this was my moment, my chance to really live what I so deeply believed and *knew* with every fiber of my being.

At that moment I felt such a trust and connection with God. Not once did I ask Him why or show anything but faith that He knew what was best. After all, this wasn't about me; it was about Chris and his time to cross.

I also realized this was a plan that had been made before Chris' birth. As his mother I had known from the moment I held him that we would come to this moment together.

What lessons were there to be learned through his death? What had his life and early passing taught me? How could I honor my son if not to remain in a state of grace and be open to his contact and the wonders and experiences now available to me?

I was not a victim, but a very important piece in the puzzle called life. Given this chance, I was going to take it. It was an opportunity. This was the first time in my life that someone I knew and loved and had taught about spirit and life after death, had crossed over.

I strongly believed there was something more and now I was determined to prove it. What could I do to best serve Chris and God and my fellow humans if not to truly be present and stand with unwavering faith that my son was still here?

Several days later, I returned home to a brand new life; one without my son, Chris. In the weeks that followed I had intended to purchase a silk floral arrangement of calla lilies for my desk at work. The bouquet was to remind me of the one my aunt had picked and that we'd brought to the accident site. Instead, I got busy with life, but continued to visualize a vase of flowers on my desk that I knew I would eventually buy.

One morning I came to work and there on my desk was a cheerful arrangement of faux calla lilies in a glass vase.

My jaw dropped. What? How? Who? I had told no one of my intention to purchase the lilies. Attached to the bouquet was a heartfelt note from a friend.

Still amazed that they had magically materialized on my desk, immediately I called my friend to thank her.

"How did you happen to choose that specific arrangement?" I asked her.

"I don't know," she replied. "Something just told me it was the arrangement to buy."

It was the one all right! I still have it five years later and not a day goes by that I don't look at the flowers and remember that lovely synchronistic manifestation.

I decided to document this experience and anything else that happened in the future that I thought was related to Chris.

Hello From Heaven

In the midst of my pain and deep sorrow, I forced myself to remain open and alert to any type of contact with Chris. I had taught him about life after death. I knew if we really did live on after we had dropped our physical body, then Chris would let me know. I felt compelled to share these contact experiences with my friends and family, even if they did not believe in life after death.

I now realized that *I was here in this lifetime to help ease the pain and fear about the transition of death.*

By opening my mind to the possibilities of something beyond our earthly domain, I was also given another gift—communication and contact with some very special divine beings, Light Beings, Messengers from God.

During the week after Chris' accident, I received a package of his personal effects from the coroner's office. Inside were his wallet, cell phone, loose change, and his watch. They were heartache in my hand as I touched each item, hoping somehow to touch and feel my son, to experience a last connection to his physical form.

I would call his phone to hear his voice message. I scrolled through his contacts and notified his friends. I would field phone calls. His phone made me feel like I still had a connection to him. Three times in two days his cell rang and I answered to silence on the other end, but always with a feeling that someone was listening, someone was there.

I knew in my heart that it was Chris trying to communicate with me. When I dialed the number shown on the phone, a voice recording would tell me *this number has been disconnected.*

Hmmm… I smiled. At least he was trying.

You Light Up My Life

Less than two weeks after Chris' accident, as I sat at my desk at home one evening, suddenly I felt his presence in the room. I couldn't see him, but I definitely knew he was there. I was cautiously excited. *It was finally happening!*

This was the beginning of numerous contact opportunities I would have with him.

I spoke aloud and told him I knew he was there. Then, jokingly I asked him to humor his mother and let me know in some physical way that he was present. I suggested turning off my computer or flicking the lights. As pure energy, I knew the easiest way for our family and friends who have crossed over to communicate with us is through the use of electricity.

To my dismay, nothing happened. I guess I had expected and wanted an instantaneous answer. Still hopeful that something would happen, I went to bed excited that I had felt his presence in the living room and knowing at some point he would humor me.

The next morning I was vacuuming in the hallway by the laundry room when one of the hallway flood lights went out. I admit that I dropped a minor expletive at my first thought of having to drag out the ladder and change a light bulb. Then, as I glanced towards the ceiling I realized that both hallway flood lights were out. It was odd that both bulbs should burn out at once, I thought. I wondered if Chris had had something to do with it.

Since I am a practical person, I flipped off the switch and then turned it on again, just to check. Instantly, both lights lit.

A smile crossed my face as joy filled my heart. I certainly

had NOT turned off those lights. It had been Chris. He had heard my request last night.

I did a little dance of joy, thanked him and then hurried to my cell phone to call my friends and family. That one moment of magic filled my entire day with excitement and possibilities. I was walking on air—and I wanted more!

Kuan Yin

That evening, my eleven-year-old daughter, Olivia, came to me too frightened to sleep in her own room. The story of the flickering lights that morning had unsettled her, so I allowed her to crawl into bed next to me. In my nightstand drawer I had placed the small book of spiritual prayers that I'd given to Chris years earlier. I found it in his nightstand drawer the weekend of his death when we cleaned out his room.

I cradled the worn dog-eared pages against my heart for a moment as if somehow they would help me gain a small connection to him. Then I read aloud for twenty minutes, sometimes repeating the same verse over and over, more for my own well-being than for my daughter's, I suppose.

Even though my first thought as a mother was to comfort and calm my little girl, I soon found myself melding with the words. They came alive on the page, their meaning tangible as they rolled off my tongue until my daughter drifted off to sleep and my lids grew weary. I fell asleep remembering the excitement of the lights in the laundry room that morning and the anticipation of another contact with my son.

In the middle of the night I awoke abruptly, adrenaline pumping full strength through my body.

Someone was in my room. Terrified, I lay on my right side with both hands tucked beneath my cheek and peered from the blankets that partially covered my head. I tried to move but was paralyzed.

Olivia lay next to me, still asleep. I couldn't even turn my head to see who might be standing next to her, much less try to save our lives.

I lay motionless and listened intently for sounds of the intruder. My mind raced with what to do next.

As I stared past my nightstand to the narrow wall at the entrance to my bathroom, I noticed a small gathering of glittering white lights. I blinked to focus on what I was seeing. Was I awake or dreaming? I pinched my palm. I was awake.

The glittering white lights were dancing on my wall in an area the size of a dinner plate. They reminded me of strong sunlight on rippling water, although I didn't need to squint from their brightness to see them. I held my breath as they performed their shimmering dance and watched as they shifted from silver to gold. It was like watching the dazzling gold glitters from Fourth of July fireworks.

As I lay quietly watching the glittering gold lights, I forgot about a possible intruder. Now the lights turned from gold to sparkling translucent red chips about the size of a deck of cards. They encompassed the entire 4 x 9 foot wall.

I was mesmerized by the sheer wonder of it. There was no reflection from these lights anywhere else in the room.

My mind raced for an explanation. The most rational one I could come up with was that a police car with its flashing red light was in my back yard. The red light must be filtering through my blackout drapes and reflecting on the wall in front of me.

The moment I realized that scenario was impossible, fear shot through me once again.

I knew that what I was witnessing was not of this earth.

Never at any time did I feel afraid of the lights, but what I did feel was fear of the unknown. As spiritual as I thought I was, nothing had prepared me for my reaction. It was too much for me to process.

In the next instant, the sparkling red lights vanished. I lay motionless for several minutes, attempting to recall every detail of the experience.

I reached out for Olivia, breathing peacefully, and then lay awake for hours peeking out from beneath my covers. I was frightened, curious, and determined as I examined every scenario I could imagine. I was desperate for an explanation of what I had witnessed.

Ultimately I could find none other than the reality that I had been visited by Spirit. It was truly extraordinary and one of the most profound events in my life. I concluded that the lights were my son in Spirit.

The next day I was so excited, I couldn't wait to tell everyone about the lights. Some loved the story and were really excited. A small group of friends and family who had had such experiences themselves were open to such possibilities. Others, of course, thought I was nuts.

For the next six months I firmly believed it had been my son's presence in my room that night. I clung to that belief until I came upon a book by Doreen Virtue, Ph.D., titled *Archangels and Ascended Masters*. Casually I flipped through the pages and stopped when I came to a section about the Eastern Goddess named Kuan Yin.

I began to read. I had no idea who Kuan Yin was and had never heard of her before now:

> She is one of the most beloved and popular Goddesses of compassion and protection, and her name means "She who hears prayers." You may see the color red when she's around, such as red sparkles of light or a red mist that appears out of nowhere.

At that moment I realized it had been Kuan Yin who had visited me with her sparkling red lights, after I had delivered my heart-felt prayers.

It had been twelve days since Chris had crossed over. As a mother I was still in a state of disbelief and shock. Waves of sadness washed over me as I contemplated never seeing or touching his physical form again. I allowed those moments to rise, crest and recede, sometimes rushing them along because the thought of another moment of contact with my son brought relief and light and joy.

My whole body tingled for months as I seemed to be half caught between worlds. It was that "walking on air" feeling that nothing can touch you and everything else before that time seemed dull and void of life.

I was floating somewhere above our human earthly existence, but not quite in the other one.

Then on March 3, 2006, a month after Chris' crossing, I walked to the laundry room through the hallway and flipped on the light switch. One of the flood lights in the ceiling turned on but not to its full strength. Then it grew brighter, dimmed once again, and grew brighter, then dimmer. The other flood light flickered.

I watched in amazement. Okay, now he was showing off! In my forty-seven years on this earth I had never seen lights do this. Immediately I knew Chris was present. I was excited and thanked him again for letting me know he was there with me.

Once again I called my close friends and family. I even called a few of the eye rolling skeptics. Their reaction never deterred me because I knew that some part of them was listening. That part needed my reinforcement that there truly was more to death than a final ending.

"Hi" In The Clouds

The night of February 25, 2006 I had my first sleep-state ADC dream about my son. I was at my mom's house in Reno where I had grown up. This was the house Chris said would always be his home. All my living relatives were arriving to express their condolences.

As I passed from room to room, people were deep in quiet whispers. I couldn't understand why everyone was so sad when I was excited and happy for my son because I knew how wonderful The Other Side was.

I knew Chris had only dropped his body and was in spirit form, but no one seemed to understand. I tried to tell them and kept saying to myself, "Don't they get it?"

What I needed was proof.

Stepping outside to the patio, I walked around to the back of the house until I reached the driveway near our fenced orchard. My mom and brother, Bill were standing there talking softly. I glanced up at the brilliant blue sky. A few large clouds were scattered about.

In one big voluminous cloud was an opening. Streaming across this opening was a glittering gold ticker tape displaying the names of all our relatives who had crossed. I remembered seeing some of those names once or twice on our ancestor chart, but would not have been able to recall them even if you paid me. I could hear their voices cheering and chattering excitedly.

"Chris is here! He's okay!" they were saying.

Their excitement about Chris' arrival filled me with joy and confirmed my knowing that there really was so much more to this existence than we have been led to believe.

I grabbed my brother, Bill and pointed to the sky. "Look! Can you see it? It's amazing. See? I told you!"

Bill looked up and squinted, but shook his head. "Where? I don't see anything!"

I turned to my mother. "Mom, look! Chris is okay. He's with all of them. Can't you see? Can't you hear them?"

She didn't even try to look up. Letting out a deep sigh, she bowed her head, her shoulders curling inward to protect her heart. "No, Shelly. I don't," she said.

Mom seemed so lost and alone. She had always said she wouldn't know what to do if she lost my brother, Bill or my son, Chris. I felt so sad for both of them. I looked up again and waved at the entire group of relatives who had already crossed over.

Despite my mother's sadness, my own heart was full of love and joy. My son was home and he was safe.

The next morning I called my mom and related my ADC dream of the night before. "Mom, in the dream, I got the distinct impression that you don't believe in life after death, that once they put your body in the ground, it's the end."

I also told her I felt she really believed that when her father, mother and brother died they had abandoned her and left her here, alone.

She started to cry. "Yes, that's exactly what I believe."

I was stunned. I had never thought to question my mother's beliefs about death, but I had been shown in my after-death communication exactly how she felt. Now she was confirming the information I had been given.

Her feelings didn't deter me; in fact, I realized that through my son I could give my mother and family hope that there was something more than this life. I decided that I was still going to relay my experiences with Chris and continue to talk about life after death, no matter how crazy they thought I was.

I do want the reader to know that it can be very difficult having these connections and sharing the experience, only to be told that you are delusional or being ridiculous, or that it's just your imagination.

Some people seem to suck the energy and magic out of a special experience. I suggest that you use your power of discernment when choosing those with whom you share your experiences.

Take Me In Your Arms

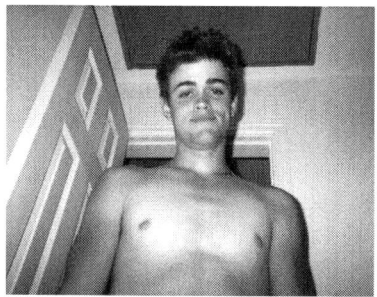

It had been a few weeks since Chris' accident. I was sitting at my desk in the living room one evening, paying bills. On my computer monitor the screen saver flashed random family pictures at five to six second intervals. I wasn't really paying attention to them, but I was aware of each picture and the instant memories of the people and places that would flash though my mind.

I noticed a picture of Chris that appeared and then stuck on the screen. I looked up, then went back to my bills several times before I sat back in my chair and stared at the screen.

Chris stared back at me. The screen had frozen. He was bare-chested and leaning slightly forward with a knowing smile. He seemed to be experiencing some secret joy and waiting for me to "get it."

Suddenly the energy in the room shifted. The air was charged and the lighting was different. He was there with me. I could feel him.

I whispered aloud, "Chris, you're here."

Instantly, I felt someone gently wrap a blanket of warmth around me. Then as if someone had poured thick warm syrup through a hole in the top of my head, the warmth slowly spread downward until it filled my entire being. I felt like I was bathing in love and peace and comfort, all at once. It was incredible.

I sat there long after the warmth had disappeared. My heart swelled with love and gratitude that I had been given this beautiful experience. I *know* that Chris had wrapped his arms around me and kissed the top of my head. Now, whenever I see that particular picture I envision the stars behind him and a set of angel wings.

Hummingbird

Three weeks after the death of my son I was organizing some of his belongings in my garage and crying as memories of him flooded my mind. My heart burst from a thousand stab wounds of loss as I carefully opened each box and began to touch and sort his things. Some were ordinary everyday things and others were precious childhood treasures. All of these items conjured memories that swirled around me.

Alone with my pain, I stopped for a moment and closed my eyes in grief and sadness and loss. My son had left behind a five-year-old little boy, Logan, and my pain was mostly for the father he would never know.

I should save some of Chris' things for Logan, I thought, *so that he too can one day touch Chris from a distance.* I opened my eyes and exhaled as tears fell unchecked from my cheeks to the concrete floor below.

Suddenly, a hummingbird darted halfway into the garage where I was standing and hovered three feet in front of me at eye level. I was startled by his presence as I watched the high speed flutter of his wings, his tiny size and beautiful iridescent green coat. He stared right at me as if his only purpose was to capture my attention and hold it.

I was enveloped by a strange calmness, a presence that instantly stole the heartache and sadness from my being. The air seemed charged as if I could actually feel it touching me and filling my lungs with a dense, tingly electrical current that penetrated every cell in my body.

What was happening? Then I felt the presence of my son. He was there with me, surrounding me in every atom and molecule that made up that space. Goose bumps exploded on my skin, wave upon wave across my arms and legs. I was compelled to speak aloud.

"Chris?" I whispered. "You're here."

A smile tugged at the corners of my mouth, lifting my heart and spirit. At the exact moment of the shifting of my mood from darkness to light, hopeless to hopeful, the tiny bird darted away, taking with him my tears and melancholy.

It was truly a miracle, I thought as I returned to my task, lighter in spirit, my heart filled with joy and gratitude.

I had always known there was so much more to this dying business than I had been told. Although I couldn't physically see Chris, I could feel him and I knew beyond a doubt that he was there with me. That experience whetted my appetite. I wanted more.

I carried that moment with me, a weapon of sorts, or a shield. Whenever I could feel myself edging towards that gaping hole that was always to my left and just a few inches from a misstep—ready to swallow me if I let it—I would pull it out to savor it and hold it close.

I'm a fighter. Although at times I may get uncomfortably

close to the crevasse, I will not let myself fall…not there… not ever. If I do, I will have lost hope and faith and the unfailing knowing that I have had since childhood that what we see in this life is just a small part of our vast experience as Spirit.

Just A Quick Hello

The first time I met my son in a sleep-state ADC came a few months after his crossing. In the dream, I was in my car driving slowly down a crowded street similar to Main Street in Disneyland. Glancing to my left out the side window, I saw Chris about fifty feet away.

Wearing a black football jersey with white numbers, he was walking in the opposite direction and carrying a tray of food as if he had just purchased something from a cafeteria.

I saw my fist pound on the window as I called out to him, but he couldn't hear me.

Reaching down, I watched my hand fumble for the window button to lower the glass. I called out and waved to him.

"Hey, Chris! Chris!"

I was so excited. I couldn't believe I was finally seeing him. He turned his head towards me as he continued to walk, then raised his eyebrows and with a half smile, made that quick chin lift gesture that people often do to acknowledge you without having to say anything.

Then, to my utter disappointment he continued on his way as if it was no big deal and he'd see me later.

What the heck? He didn't even stop to say hello? I was in a state of disbelief and deeply disappointed that nothing more had passed between us.

It was such a short and simple moment, but as I look back, it was exactly like our relationship in life. He would pop in briefly, say hi, and then be on his way.

9

Mandi's Story

Special Delivery

A few weeks after the accident, Chris' uncle Peter called me and asked what my initials were. I told Peter they were M.P. He said he had something really cool for me that he'd found while packing up Chris' apartment. It was a handmade dish on his nightstand that said, "C.A. + M.P. Forever."

I hadn't known about this dish, but it was obvious that Chris had made it years ago. I was so overwhelmed at that moment by the love I felt coming from Chris. It was such a beautiful and loving present, a symbol of our lasting love and friendship. I still cherish it to this day.

Within weeks after Chris' crossing, I received a call from Kristin, Chris' little sister. She told me that Chris had visited her in a dream and was insisting that she give me his favorite T-shirt. He told her, "Kristin, you already have a bunch of my clothes, so send this one to Mandi because she needs it."

When Kristen told me this, I began to laugh and thought to myself that Chris was still letting all of us know that he's here. Kristen did as Chris directed and sent me the shirt. It was so sweet of her to give up something she loved.

Hug Me Hello

The next few weeks after the accident were very difficult. It was an up and down rollercoaster of emotions for me.

I could hardly talk about Chris without bursting into tears. It was during this time that I had my first ADC with him. In this dream, Aric and Chris had just returned home from snowboarding, which is something I had always wished they could do together [Aric and Chris had never met]. I was in the kitchen making dinner and talking to Chris.

He said that he thought the world of Aric and knew he was a great guy. He also told me he thought that Aric was the one for me and he was so happy knowing I was with someone who would treat me well. He told me that he loved me and he would always be there for me. I told him how much I appreciated what he'd said about Aric. Then I told him that I loved him too, and we hugged.

I awoke with chills all over my body. This had been the most realistic dream I'd ever had. I actually felt Chris hug me. It was more than a dream. Chris had come to visit me.

Many times in the last few years I have felt Chris around me. There have been times when I'm vacuuming my house and just thinking about him. As I get lost in my thoughts, I can feel a tap on my shoulder. I always jump with surprise and then I say out loud, "Chris, what the heck!"

I think he enjoys watching me jump, and I enjoy knowing he's there. Just as he was always kidding and messing with me when he was alive, he still pulls his crazy tricks on me from The Other Side.

Shelly's Story

Out Of The Mouths Of Babes

Logan and Chris, Dallas 2005

I chose to have a Celebration of Life ceremony around the time of Chris' birthday in June instead of a funeral right after his death. I wanted to put some distance between the accident and the service, mainly because wounds would have begun to heal.

The house where I had grown up and where Chris had spent much time as a child and adult was perfect. My mother's house was filled with memories. She bought a delightful fountain for the garden in the back patio. "Chris' fountain," she calls it. Birds love to bathe in the different tiers, with tall stalks of zinnias and peonies blooming beneath its bottom bowl.

The back yard seemed as large as a football field. I can still see Chris and Kristin playing outside as children in the deep green grass. A giant rope that hung from an old elm tree was a favorite pastime for them. The day of the ceremony I was watching Chris' son, Logan, swinging back and forth with an occasional running push from me.

"Grammy, do you miss my dad?" he asked out of the blue.

"Yes, I do." I smiled. "But I know he's right here with us, honey."

"I know he is too," he said triumphantly. "And I'm gonna swing right through him!"

My heart sang with the sweetness of the moment and the knowledge that Logan had been able to see his dad. No one had discussed with Logan the possibility of seeing his dad after the accident. His mother, Samantha, really didn't believe in any of it and since they lived in Texas, I hadn't been able to talk with Logan about it.

I received a phone call a few weeks later. Samantha was tucking Logan into bed and leaned forward to kiss him goodnight. After the kiss he asked her to give one to his daddy too. Samantha leaned forward and kissed the air.

Logan frowned and said, "Not there, Mom! He's sitting on the end of the bed."

A Nudge From Spirit

I did a lot of thinking about Chris' ceremony. Whom should I invite, who would preside, what would be said, what prayers would be read? One book instantly popped into my mind: *Jonathan Livingston Seagull*, by Richard Bach. I'd read it thirty years ago at my dad's suggestion, and it had always stayed with me.

Spirit was sending me a clear message that I needed to read it again. I promised myself to pick up a copy as soon as possible. Yet despite being on my mind daily, somehow I never got around to purchasing it.

Three months passed and I flew to Reno with Olivia, my youngest daughter, several days before the ceremony. I brought my son's ashes to spread later on Mount Rose at his request, but I didn't want Olivia and Kristin to see the box. My mom had suggested hiding it in her bedroom on top of her file cabinets. I agreed. Who would notice it there?

Mom had a large bedroom with a full office area. Anyone who had seen it knows of the accumulated clutter. None of us in our right mind dared venture into it. Hiding the box would just be a matter of setting it on top of a pile somewhere.

Carefully I worked my way through the maze of stuff on the floor and spotted a likely resting place for the package. Reaching up on my tiptoes, I placed the box on top of the tall ten foot long filing cabinet piled with books and papers. With my arms still stretched above my head, I just happened to glance down. Sitting on a pile of random books on top of a crate stuffed with papers and magazines, was the original copy of *Jonathan Livingston Seagull* that I had read thirty years ago.

No way! I declared to myself. Its faded blue cover was a sight to behold. I stared at it for a moment and then looked skyward. "Okay. I got the message," I grinned.

If I had attempted to locate that book in Mom's room it would have taken me hours. How it found its way to the top of a pile in that very spot, from the dozens of hiding places I could have chosen, I don't know—but there it was!

Cradling it in my hands, I thanked Spirit for guiding me to this precious gift.

Gone was the urgency I'd felt upon entering the room. I had been so eager to quickly hide the box and move through the numerous errands to be done before the ceremony began. The only sense of urgency I now felt was to immediately sit somewhere and reread the book.

As once again I revisited this beautiful and poignant story, tears flowed freely. I knew instantly why Spirit wanted me to find this particular book. The ceremony was an opportunity to open people's minds to new thinking—to free their hearts and minds of sadness and fear, and to show them the possibilities of something that was both great and limitless.

A few minutes later, I had chosen the passage to be read at the ceremony:

> They came in the evening, then, and found Jonathan gliding peaceful and alone through his beloved sky. The two gulls that appeared at his wings were pure as starlight, as the glow from them was gentle and friendly in the high night air. But most lovely of all was the skill with which they flew, their wingtips moving a precise and constant inch from his own.
>
> Without a word, Jonathan put them to his test, a test that no gull had ever passed. He twisted his wings, slowed to a single mile per hour above a stall. The two radiant birds slowed with him, smoothly, locked in position. They knew about slow flying.
>
> He folded his wings, rolled and dropped to a dive a hundred ninety miles per hour. They dropped with him streaking down in flawless formation.

At last he turned that speed straight up into a long vertical slow-roll. They rolled with him smiling. He recovered to level flight and was quiet for a time before he spoke. "Very well," he said, "who are you?"

"We're from your Flock, Jonathan. We are your brothers." The words were strong and calm. "We've come to take you higher, to take you home."

"Home I had none. Flock I have none. I am Outcast. And we fly now at the peak of the Great Mountain Wind. Beyond a few hundred feet I can lift this old body no higher."

"But you can, Jonathan. For you have learned. One school is finished, and the time has come for another to begin."

As it had shined across him all his life, so understanding lighted that moment for Jonathan Seagull. They were right. He *could* fly higher, and it was time to go home.

He gave one last look across the sky, across the magnificent silver land where he had learned so much.

"I am ready," he said at last.

And Jonathan Livingston Seagull rose with the two star-bright gulls to disappear into a perfect dark sky.[3]

---

3 Reprinted with the permission of Scribner, a Division of Simon & Schuster, Inc., from *Jonathan Livingston Seagull* by Richard Bach. Copyright© 1970 by Richard D. Bach and Leslie Parrish-Bach. All rights reserved.

So many people commented on the reading, many of them old enough to contemplate their own crossing. With tears in their eyes, they mentioned how much they had loved the book and how much comfort it had given them. It helped me, too, as I have always been a free spirit, cast from the flock at a young age, knowing there was so much more and yearning to learn everything I could to take me higher.

By the grace of God I have been allowed glimpses of those possibilities. I know for sure that we do not die; we just drop our bodies and live on. I had taught my son this knowing and was richly rewarded by the contact I have had with him since his crossing five years ago.

Over The Rainbow

Logan and Chris, Lake Tahoe 2001

On the evening of June 19, 2006, we celebrated my son's twenty-sixth birthday. At my mother's request, my brother, Peter had ordered a sheet cake with a rainbow. Mother added some bisque porcelain angels for decoration and spoke to Logan about angels, his father in heaven, and that he would now be able to paint rainbows for him.

You never quite know what's going through the mind of a five year old. He listened to his great-grandmother speak and was quiet and contemplative before he blew out the candles. Pulling the angels from the thick frosting, he licked them clean.

"These are my daddy's angels," he said. We were all nodding in silence, since it had just gotten too tough to speak.

A few days later, on the eve of the ceremony, I still had no plans to speak, since I knew the service was in good hands with a wonderful Reverend I had chosen. She had graciously accepted my request and I flew her in from Idaho the night before the service.

The patio was complete with a white tent with open sides, tables for eight, laced with spring green table cloths and floral arrangements. There was also an area for the gorgeous buffet the next afternoon. My mother is the consummate hostess and loves family dinners, so having one the night before a big event was easily arranged.

A dozen or so of us were sitting down to dinner outside, beneath the soft covering of the tent. It was an early summer evening and the warm golden sunlight lit the yard with an ethereal quality. The flowers appeared more radiant and the grass was alive with a myriad of green hues. Leaves fluttered gently on the trees against the slightest whisper of a breeze. Dark clouds gathered ominously in the sky to the east.

As we joined each other at the tables, our plates laden with a bountiful meal, I heard someone say, "I wonder if Chris is here."

"Yes, he is," I answered.

Suddenly, in the midst of the golden glow of a late sinking summer sun, the sky opened up. Rain pounded the top of the tent and ran in rivulets down the support poles. Spouts of water shot off the scalloped edges and splattered against the pavement. We hurried inside, all except Logan. With one hand cupped around a pole, face tilted skyward, we watched as he stood beneath a downpour off the tent, smiling in delight. He was soaked.

His mother ordered him inside, but all I could think about was how much he resembled his daddy. Chris would have done the exact same thing.

Ten minutes later the rain had stopped and off in the distance a brilliant rainbow appeared.

"Look!" Logan cried. "It's my daddy's rainbow!"

I don't think there was a dry eye among us.

"Yes, Logan," I said. "It's your daddy's rainbow."

Synchronicity is a wondrous thing. Within moments of someone asking if my son was here with us, we received an answer. Some people would say it was coincidence. I choose to call it a miracle.

Answered Prayers

The morning of the ceremony dawned clear and sunny. It was a glorious day for a celebration. The Reverend Wendy Collins arrived from her hotel and asked to take a walk with me in the garden. She wanted to discuss how I envisioned the ceremony. She mentioned that she had selected a few prayers.

We picked a garden bench near the playhouse on the far edge of the yard, to sit and talk privately. I told her I didn't think I would be able to speak. It had been four months since his crossing, but my heart and soul were raw and tender. I didn't want to cry in front of everyone. I handed her the *Jonathan Livingston Seagull* book and showed her the passages.

She held my hand and asked me to say a prayer. I'm not used to formally addressing Our Father, especially in front of a Reverend, so after a moment's hesitation I just said what was in my heart.

"Father, please give me the strength today to stand in

grace. Give me the words that will help people heal, take the pain from their hearts, and let them know that Chris is okay." There it was: simple, sweet and to the point.

Close to forty people were in attendance. The Reverend opened the ceremony with a lovely greeting and the prayer of Saint Francis. She spoke for several minutes and then asked if anyone wished to speak.

Several people shared stories of Chris and two of his friends told of his kindness and intervention in their lives at a time when they had hit bottom. One young man mentioned that without Chris' help he would have been back in jail, but now he was married with a family and great job. Mandi, a lifetime friend, soul mate, and Chris' first girlfriend, was the other speaker.

I sat quietly with my immediate family, my heart filled with gratitude and appreciation as I listened to these loving accounts of my son. Suddenly I felt the urge to speak. I stood and addressed the group and then I read the passages from *Jonathan Livingston Seagull*.

After the ceremony ended, my older daughter, Kristin, approached me with a stunned look on her face.

"Oh my God, Mom!" she whispered. "What happened to you? We were all shaking our heads. We couldn't believe it."

"What are you talking about, honey?" I asked her.

"We couldn't believe that you were able to stand up and talk like that. It was as if something came over you."

She must be right, I thought to myself. Something had taken over my body. I felt so strong and sure and the words poured out effortlessly. I had said exactly what I had prayed for earlier.

My aunt approached me and said, "That was beautiful. You missed your calling. You should have been a minister. In fact, I may want you to speak at my funeral."

I want to say that I don't know what came over me, but in fact, I do. God had heard me in the garden and sent His strength and wisdom to guide me.

Kristin's Story

Do You Get It Now?

Chris & Kristin, Lake Tahoe 2005

About a year after Chris died, I was listening to the radio. I heard the DJ say he was going to have a guest speaker, a medium, later in the week. My mom was visiting me at the time and I mentioned to her that I was going to try to win a reading. She said she thought it would be fun. Since she was returning home the following day, she told me to call her. "Let me know what the medium had to say."

Making a note on my calendar, I called the station on the appointed day to win a chance reading. After 30 minutes of continuous calling I finally got through and was able to speak with the medium directly for a few minutes. I asked him about my brother and if anything was coming through to him.

One of the most memorable things he said to me was, "Your brother is telling me he has a message for your mother. He's saying that you need to tell her, '*He gets it now.*'"

"*He gets it now?*" I repeated. "What does that mean?"

The medium said he didn't know, but the message was important and to be sure to tell my mother.

Shortly after speaking with the medium, I called my mom to tell her that Chris had spoken through the medium. "He said, '*He gets it now.*'"

For a moment my mom didn't respond and then she gasped, "Oh my God!"

She then explained that while she was visiting me earlier in the week she had walked by an 8 x 10 framed photo of Chris and me on the wall near the guest room. It was a picture of us taken at Lake Tahoe one summer and one she had never seen.

She said she stood quietly and stared at it. Feeling sentimental and sad that things had ended up the way they did, she looked at Chris in the photo and asked, "*Do you get it now? Do you understand?*" She told me she was referring to life and our spiritual connection, and how one person's decisions, good or bad, can affect so many other lives.

I had not known my mom had spoken to the picture in the hallway. Having the medium confirm that Chris had heard her question was a startling confirmation that our loved ones live on in the afterlife.

Heavenly Hands

**Kristin and Chris, April 2005
Auburn, Cord, Duesenberg Club
Great Gatsby Charity Ball**

A year after my brother died and a month before my college graduation, I found myself frustrated, angry, and crying in the parking lot of ADP, a payroll service. I had just finished my seventh interview with them and had come to the conclusion that I would rather die than spend my life selling payroll. As I sat in my car crying, I spoke to my brother. "Beanie, damn it, if you're there and you can hear me, I need your help. Please help me find work that I love. Please help me find a career where I can work outside and do something to help animals. I don't want to spend my life in an office doing things that don't inspire me. Please help me!"

After pleading to my brother for help, I dried my eyes, collected myself and drove twenty minutes north to the stable where I kept my horse. I took him out, fed him his dinner, then headed back to my car to drive home.

As I walked out of the barn I noticed a woman standing in the stall with one of the horses. She was a person I had never seen before. Just as I reached my car I heard a voice say, "Kristin, turn around and go talk to her." Although I didn't know why I needed to talk to this woman, I listened to my inner guidance and turned around.

Poking my head into the stall, I introduced myself. As we got to talking I learned she was an equine massage therapist.

An hour into our conversation she said cheerfully, "If you go to school and become a licensed massage therapist, I'll be your mentor and teach you everything you need to know about working on horses."

Inspired and enthused, I agreed wholeheartedly! The moment I got home I did my research and enrolled in a massage therapy school. Five days after my college graduation I started my first day of classes. Three and a half years later, I own my own business doing sports therapy on some of the top show horses in the country.

Thanks to my brother's help from The Other Side, my prayers were answered exactly as I had asked. I have a career I love, I'm working outside and I'm helping animals! Thank you, Beanie!!!

Shelly's Story

Golden Light Of Love

A year or so after my son's death, I started visiting an Australian shaman who lived in my town. She was a tiny woman with extremely short hair and a twinkle in her eye. I had been to several of her classes and decided I would like to do a Soul Retrieval.

A Soul Retrieval helps people gain insight into a problem and/or to locate the lost part of their souls. These parts can be missing due to physical or emotional trauma that occurs in this or other lifetimes. The Soul Retrieval helps to heal the individual.

A shaman captures the fragmented parts of us through his or her connection with spirit guides and teachers. My shaman knew nothing of my son or family, except that Chris had passed.

I was blindfolded and lay down on my back on a single bed in a quiet room. The shaman mentioned that the blindfold was for her benefit, to allow her to move freely around me without feeling conspicuous.

She chanted, drummed, danced and put herself in a trance state to enable her to contact my guides and family and to see my past.

The moment she started chanting, I felt my physical body start to sink into the bed. My soul or spirit rose several inches above my physical form. It felt as if each cell in my body were vibrating. I relaxed as best as I could and let her do her work.

I could hear voices, and at one point it felt and sounded like a giant bird with a huge wingspan had descended upon the room. I could hear and feel its presence all around me.

About a half hour later it was over and she began to tell me what she saw. It was fascinating. She described accurately both my mother's and father's personalities and my relationship with them. She also passed on information that no one else knew but me.

At one point she said my son came into the room, grasped my hand and gently kissed the back of it. He said to her, "You know, my mom always knows when I'm in the car with her." It's true. I do know when Chris is in the car with me.

While driving, I often get a strong sense of my son's presence followed immediately by hearing the song on the radio that reminds me of him. During those moments I always have the urge to lay my right arm, with my palm upwards, across the armrest. I never questioned those urges but just went with them. I knew every time this happened that Chris was sitting next to me holding my hand.

After we finished the session, it was time to pick up Olivia at the elementary school. As I was driving along, suddenly I felt my heart chakra[4] open wide and connect with Divine Love. I had a vision in my mind's eye of Jesus surrounded with a luminous aura of love and golden light. It was as if I had a direct link to Jesus and He offered the unconditional love that one feels in His presence.

---

4 Chakra - A spinning ball of colored energy located in one of the seven spiritual centers of the human body.

The only way I can describe it is to imagine a ten-inch round river of golden light brighter than the sun, starting at the center of the chest and connecting to His entire being. It was so filled with the most extraordinary love, tears of absolute joy and exaltation ran down my cheeks. For the next twenty minutes, I found myself in a state of grace with the highest form of Love filling every part of me. I felt so warm and safe, cradled in this Love. Somehow I managed to end up safely in the school parking lot. I surely don't remember most of the drive.

During this event I had an epiphany. I realized that all my life I had been seeking that specific love with a man, and none of these relationships had ended well. I also realized that no man on earth is capable of that love. It was a Divine Love and the experience meant that I had unknowingly been searching for it all this time. I had *remembered* what it felt like to be in the presence of Jesus and connected with Divine Love. I had memories of being on The Other Side. This was proof to me, personally, that *we do not die!*

All Aboard

In my second sleep-state ADC, I was walking through an enormous transportation center with a huge train platform and rows of track as well as runways for planes. People were scurrying everywhere carrying luggage and rushing towards departure gates. The colors of the center were varying shades of grey.

I followed the crowd for awhile and then suddenly I had a sense that someone was behind me.

I turned around. It was Chris.

"Oh my God! Chris, you're here?!" I exclaimed breathlessly.

"Yeah," he shrugged. "I just had to go away for a little while," he added in a matter-of-fact tone.

I was stunned. I couldn't believe it was Chris. I turned away for a moment to see if anyone else noticed he was standing there with me, as real as everyone else. Then when I looked back, he was gone.

Once again I felt frustrated and at a loss for answers to the numerous questions I had for him. Why was he always just appearing for a brief moment, cool, calm and collected—and so nonchalant? Nothing urgent in his appearance, just the same laid-back child I'd always known him to be. As in life, so in death, I suppose.

Keep Your Eyes On The Road

In the fall of 2007 I was waiting at a red light across the street from my house. I had just finished grocery shopping and Olivia had texted me from home, asking me when was I coming back. I sat at the red light with a car next to me in the left turn lane. All I needed to do was cross the intersection to get to the entrance to my neighborhood.

The light turned green, but I hadn't finished texting my answer to Olivia. I crept forward slowly into the four lane intersection. A westbound car to my upper right stopped at the light in the fast lane. The lane next to him was vacant.

I had barely reached the median, still texting, when I heard my son's voice say to me from the back seat, "You'd better watch out! You're gonna get T-boned!"

I looked up just in time to see a car run the westbound red light at about 60mph. I was startled and shocked as I slammed on the brakes. My son had saved my life or saved me from a major injury. Thank you, Chris. I'm so glad to know that you're watching out for me.

I See The Light

Light Being - similar to the one in October 2007

In late October of 2007 I awoke in the middle of the night to turn up the thermostat. It had gotten colder outside, which is typical of high desert climate in the late fall, and I had only a light covering on the bed.

Flipping on the hall light, I made my way to the laundry room, adjusted the temperature setting and sleepily headed back to my bedroom.

As I turned off the hall light, suddenly I saw before me in the bedroom a solid ball of brilliant white light. It was larger than a ping-pong ball, situated three feet from the ceiling and about three feet out from the wall.

I froze in my tracks and watched as it zipped to my left, parallel to the wall, took a sharp left, then zipped parallel to that wall for about five feet before it disappeared. Following in its wake was a trail of light similar to that of a twirling Fourth of July sparkler.

It all happened so fast. My immediate thought was of a burglar with a flashlight outside my bedroom window. Then I remembered I had blackout curtains on my sliding door and the light had started on the same solid wall as the curtains.

At once I patrolled the house, checking all the locks before returning to bed.

I lay awake, pondering what exactly it was that I had seen. Did it have anything to do with Chris?

The next morning I related the event to a girlfriend who lived nearby in the desert.

She simply said, "That was a Light Being."

"A Light Being?" I repeated incredulously. "What's that?"

"A Light Being can be any of the following," she said. "It can be an emanation from Spirit, an inter-dimensional being, a guide, angel, or extraterrestrial. Who really knows for sure? But they are here to help us."

She told me that the International Orb and Light Being Convention was scheduled in November at the Palm Springs Convention Center.

"Are you kidding me?" I asked as I rolled my eyes. "An Orb Convention?" I knew what an orb was, and although I have always been an open-minded person, I hadn't heard the term Light Being. If I saw this little being with my own eyes, there must be a reason. This was more than coincidence, I concluded. I wanted to know if there was any correlation between the appearance of the orb or Light Being in my bedroom and my son. I took the event as my personal invitation to attend the convention.

That afternoon I registered online. Two weeks later I drove to Palm Springs filled with questions and excited to learn about Light Beings.

When I arrived at the Palm Springs Convention Center it was deserted. Had I gotten the wrong place? Maybe I had arrived on the wrong day. I circled the entire city block looking for some sign of life. I honestly thought for a moment that everyone was beamed up without me.

I parked my car and ventured towards the glass entry doors to look for information regarding the convention, when I noticed another puzzled soul. We stopped to talk for a moment. I then contacted my girlfriend who got on the Internet and learned that the Orb and Light Being Convention had been postponed until March of 2008 due to the large California wildfires. Since I had registered so late, I hadn't been added to their email list for notification.

I relayed the information to the woman I had stopped to talk with and then made the suggestion that we go for coffee, since it was early morning.

It's astonishing how life works. I learned that this woman's name was Dawn Spitz. She was not only interesting to talk with; she also happened to be the President of the Palm Springs Writers Guild. I was passionate about writing, but needed some direction and encouragement. There is a Buddhist saying that I've heard through the years: "When the student is ready, the teacher will come." It's true.

I returned home later that morning and researched orbs and Light Beings on the Internet. I had a few photos myself that contained orbs. These had been taken immediately after Chris' accident when Logan and his mother, Samantha, came to visit. Among my collection I also found pictures with orbs pre-dating Chris' death, including a picture of my son and me surrounded by these Light Beings. I thought they were interesting, but didn't begin to seriously photograph them until the spring of 2009.

That year, we attended my uncle's funeral reception at the Los Angeles Country Club. It was a lovely event and I became the "official photographer." I documented the event with friends and family attending, but I had a secondary motive. I wanted to see if any orbs were present.

I soon discovered the orbs were everywhere. I was so excited and tried to enlighten my relatives of their presence. Since that time I have learned they are appearing in digital photos to millions of people around the world. I don't believe these Light Beings are ghostly apparitions; rather, I believe that some of them are the essence of who we are when we are out of body. They are our family, friends, guides and angels that watch over and help us on a daily basis.

Ask And You Shall Receive

On January 16, 2008 I was in our new house unpacking some clothing in the master bedroom. The moving van had not yet arrived and only a few boxes were stacked in the room. I wondered to myself if Chris knew I had moved. The spiritual side of me jumped in and I chided myself with, "Of course he knows, Silly!"

Instantly, I heard a strange thrumming noise. After ignoring it for several minutes, I went to investigate. A hummingbird had flown in through the open crack of the sliding door and was trying to escape through one of the four large picture windows in the family room.

I had no way of guiding him down the high wall and out through the door. I certainly didn't want to traumatize him by waving my arms and possibly chasing him around the great room in an effort to send him outside. What should I do?

Suddenly I felt compelled to start walking towards him. He was still fluttering, unsuccessful in his attempt to escape through the window. Since I thought my presence might frighten him, I stopped ten feet back from the window. Then, as if guided by some unseen force, I stretched my palm into the air as high as it would go and closed my eyes.

To my utter amazement, it lighted on my fingertips. My breath caught, my heart fluttered and time stood still. Slowly I lowered my hand and gazed in awe at the tiny, almost weightless creature before me. He was magnificent. I drank in the iridescent green of his coat, his dainty head and long beak, his tiny spider-like feet, one on the tip of my index finger and one on my middle finger.

"You're beautiful," I whispered. "Oh... my... God! Look at you!"

My little friend cocked his head this way and that as if he understood and appreciated my heartfelt compliment. He appeared completely relaxed and calm as if he knew this was exactly what he was supposed to do and where he was supposed to be. I was caught up in the wonder of the moment—his presence, his beauty, the miracle in my hand—when suddenly thoughts of my son filled my mind.

Instantly, I felt the energy in the room shift as if the very air itself were charged with a strange electrical current. Goose bumps exploded on my body. Then I felt him. Chris was everywhere: in the air and sunlight that poured though the windows, beneath my feet, touching my skin.

I had to ask, even though I already knew, "Chris, is that you, buddy? You're here, aren't you?"

I knew he was. I knew it in my gut and in my heart and in every fiber of my being. I knew he was behind this little miracle. Not that he was the bird, but it was his way of letting me know that no matter where I lived, he would always be with me.

My heart sang and my spirit soared. My love spilled forth, filling the room around me.

Life is fascinating and so much, much more than I had ever been taught.

The tiny bird was still patiently perched on my fingertips—a miracle messenger. I felt so small and insignificant in this incredible experience, yet I was so grateful to be part of it…so grateful that as a mother I could ask a heartfelt question of my son and instantly receive confirmation that he had heard me.

Once more I focused on the mission at hand: getting the little bird safely out the door. With the stealth of a cat, I crossed the room, the bird still perched on my fingertips. Slowly and gracefully I made my way to the door. If only

I'd opened it more than twelve inches earlier that morning! Holding my breath, I prayed I would be able to slip through the opening without disturbing him.

Success! Now I was in for another surprise. Once I had stepped outside, I assumed the hummingbird would fly away. Instead, I was dumbfounded to find him still content to stay perched on my fingertips. He was looking around, but obviously waiting for something to happen.

The silence stretched between us as I studied him once again, this little creature of God, a messenger, a miracle.

He continued to rest on my fingertips long enough to make me question whether or not he would actually fly away. Next, I did what any rational person would do with a tiny hummingbird perched on their fingers. I spoke to him.

"I am so glad you came to visit me today," I cooed. "You are welcome to come back any time."

We stared at each other silently for a moment. I had the distinct feeling that he was waiting for something else as he glanced around patiently and waited for me to figure it out. *But what?*

Maybe I was supposed to tell him it was okay to leave. I thought about this for a moment. How absurd that seemed.

Yet, my intuition nudged me to speak to him, so I did.

"I'll be okay, little one. You can go now."

With that, he looked me straight in the eye, nodded his head and disappeared into the brilliant blue sky.

I staggered backward a step or two with my mouth agape and my hand on my heart. *What in the world had just happened?*

I stood there imprinting every detail to memory, soaking

in the magic and grateful for the moment, grateful for the knowledge that my son was here with me.

What the heck! No one would believe this!

I had to tell somebody so I dialed my girlfriend and then my older daughter and breathlessly relayed the event. To this day those precious moments are as vivid and real as the instant they happened.

The memory of this experience always lightens my heart and reminds me to look for the possibility of an instant miracle from our loved ones on The Other Side.

Be Careful What You Ask For

Thanksgiving 2008 was a huge, extended family gathering with nearly sixty relatives. The family was celebrating another special event; my aunt was turning eighty. My mother planned a wonderful few days with meals at two different local family members' homes and several dinners, including Thanksgiving, at her home. Since so many people would be wandering around and hired help coming in and out, I decided to put my wallet out of the way for the duration of my stay.

The night before my flight home I couldn't remember where I had hidden it. I tore the house upside down, retraced my steps and practically pulled my hair out looking for it. I needed my identification to board the plane!

Once again I headed towards the master bedroom and my dad's dressing room, searching the area.

Frustrated, I raised my voice and demanded that my son, Chris, help me find it. I had always heard you can ask for help, and now I did.

I waited a minute or two, but nothing happened.

Irritated with myself for my little tantrum demanding instant help from above, I continued my search. As soon as I reached the threshold of the master bedroom door, I stopped and was suddenly forced to stand at attention. I felt as if someone had me by the shoulders. They marched me down the hall. When I reached the office door, which was my bedroom when I was growing up, I halted and did a military precision 90 degree turn to the left. I took three steps, halted again, executed another 90 degree turn to the left, and then felt my head shoved forward into a wire basket holding papers—and my wallet!

Holy Cow! *Did that just really happen?* I stood there dumbfounded for a minute and then sheepishly smiled and shook my head. I thanked my son and apologized for my bad behavior. His ability to connect with me from The Other Side never ceases to amaze me.

Give Me A Sign

In May of 2009 after an exhausting four months of remodeling, I moved into what I hoped was "the-rest-of-my-life's-home." I had moved twelve times in twenty years and was anxious to unpack, settle in and decorate my space.

A year later, I was home enjoying a pleasant morning in the California desert. I had opened my front and back doors to let in the fresh air and the sweet scent of alyssum drifted in on the breeze.

I sat down on the couch in the family room for a minute to relax and enjoy the moment. I thought of my son, Chris and wondered what he was up to today on The Other Side.

I knew I didn't need to ask him if he was aware that I'd moved again, but I was wondering why nothing notable had happened yet in this house to tell me he was here. After all, it was my Forever Home.

All of a sudden, a hummingbird flew in the front door towards me, circled the kitchen several times, and landed on the back of one of my kitchen chairs.

I giggled with pure joy at the timing and at once grabbed my cell phone to take a picture. He sat there for several minutes, very content and paying no attention to the wide open door ten feet away.

When I began to wonder if he would leave, he took flight, zoomed around my family room and sped into the dining room. The little bird landed on the black window frame that separated the top stationary glass pane from the bottom sliding glass pane. It was a bit of an awkward position for him, but he seemed in no hurry to leave my home. The thought crossed my mind to put my hand out again, but what were the chances of the bird landing there a second time? I went to the broom closet and grabbed a broom. Moving slowly, I maneuvered the broom just beneath him.

All he had to do was step off the frame and onto the broom if he so desired, and I could take him outside to freedom.

Much to my surprise, that's exactly what he did. He hopped onto the broom and I carried him through the dining room, family room, entry hall and outside to the courtyard. He disappeared instantly into the flawless blue desert sky.

Chris again! It was not a coincidence, but a synchronistic event where thought and form fell effortlessly into place.

What reason did the bird have to fly into my house and

chill on the back of my kitchen chair? For that matter, why did he hitch a ride on a broom when he could have just as easily and more instinctively flown off and out either of the two wide open doors?

I try not to analyze these things anymore. They are what they are and I'm grateful for every new experience. We are all part of the never ending circle of life, connected by the eternal, brilliant, Divine Light in each of us.

What Spirit Wants

Logan   Chris

A year after our chance meeting at the postponed Orb Convention, I received a phone call from Dawn Spitz asking if I might consider taking over the position of Vice President of Membership of the Palm Springs Writers Guild. I said yes and spent the next two years performing the duties of that position.

I enjoyed getting to know everyone, especially the board members. They are a group of hard working, dedicated volunteers who truly make that organization run smoothly.

In December of 2010, I received an email announcing registration for the First Annual AfterLife Awareness Conference in Phoenix, Arizona at the end of April 2011. The foremost authorities in the fields of Near-Death Experience, Out-of-Body Experience and After-Death Communication would be gathering and presenting at the conference.

Needless to say, I was excited to participate but decided to postpone my registration until March, assuming there would be plenty of time to purchase a ticket. I told everyone I would be attending and was looking forward to the workshops and lectures.

Much to my dismay, they closed the registration in early January. They had sold out! I was so disappointed. I guess it just wasn't meant to be, I told myself.

"I leave it up to you," I said to Chris, and placed my name on the waiting list.

The conference got me thinking. I decided it was time to finally write a book about my after-death communication with Chris.

I was in no hurry and had no deadline, but I knew in my gut that this was a work that had to be written. My intention wasn't to heal myself, per se, but to share my story with others, hoping it might ease their pain if they had experienced similar losses.

In January I spent two weeks working on the manuscript, feeling excited and motivated. Then suddenly I fell into a deep depression.

I had never felt like this before. Was I reliving Chris' accident through my writing? Was it because the five-year anniversary of his crossing loomed in front of me on February 4? Maybe both; I'm not sure.

As I continued to write down these moving experiences, I fell deeper into a place I had yet to venture. It was the hole

I had mentioned earlier in the book that was always to my left, just inches from a misstep.

At a certain point I stopped writing and moped about the house in my pajamas, not leaving for days at a time. I didn't tell my family how I felt, although my youngest daughter, Olivia noticed. The pain was overwhelming and debilitating. I just didn't want to be here anymore. It hurt too much.

I was so deeply and profoundly sad. I missed seeing my son in person. I'd had five years to watch the aftermath of his devastating accident unfold in front of me and had spent part of last summer taking care of Logan, Chris' son and my only grandchild. It was the first time I had really been able to spend any quality time with him.

It was as if I were reliving those days with Chris when he was a little boy. I made his lunch and took him to his year-round school. I helped with homework and got him showered and into bed. We played ping-pong every day for a month. We took Orb pictures at night before bed.

The experience was bittersweet. I fought back tears as I sat on the sidelines of Logan's football practice, aching for the little boy who would give anything to see his dad sitting there instead of me.

I spent all of February in a very dark place. My college girlfriend, Sherie Early, turned on the lights and helped me though that time. We talked often by phone, since she lives in Reno near my family. She is a wise, loving, and beautiful person and through all the years, I am so grateful to still have her as my friend.

At the beginning of March, another friend talked me into taking a yoga class with her. It had been twenty years since my last yoga class, but finally I felt well enough to leave the house. Somehow I had climbed out of the hole. On my way to class that evening, my cell phone rang.

It was Terri Daniel, organizer of the AfterLife Awareness Conference, calling to tell me there was one cancellation and my name was on the waiting list. Did I want the ticket?

Absolutely.

Suddenly, I was on fire. I knew I wanted to have my published book in hand when I landed in Phoenix on April 29, 2011. But could it be done?

I contacted Mark E. Anderson, the current president of the Palm Springs Writers Guild, who is also a Book Shepherd—someone who guides writers through the process of planning and producing a book.

I shared my plan with Mark and as luck would have it or Spirit planned it, he was available. So was John Carrigan, copy editor, and Vicki Mills, book publisher and mentor. Both were also Palm Springs Writers Guild Board members. Everything fell into place.

13

Mandi's Story

The Power Of Prayer

Mandi and Chris at the prom

Aric has been a mixed martial artist most of his life and in recent years he started to compete in cage fights. In January of 2010, he was offered a title shot in his weight class at the largest event in Idaho. Aric is an extremely talented martial artist. All of us knew he not only deserved this shot, but also that he would win. There was no doubt in any of our minds.

He trained every day for weeks to prepare for this fight. The week before his fight he was having a hard time and was really beginning to doubt his abilities. Did he actually deserve the opportunity to fight for the title?

For the entire week he was distant and depressed. His friends and I tried to talk to him, to no avail.

It was Wednesday, the day before Aric would travel to the weigh-in for the event. I could tell he was upset and nothing I said seemed to help. Later that day when I was alone, I talked to Chris and asked him for his help.

"Chris, please give Aric the strength to get through his fight, and also help him once more to have faith in his own abilities."

The following day, Aric left for the weigh-in. On February 5, Friday night, a group of friends and family went to watch him compete. I was so nervous for him. I knew he could win as long as he stayed focused.

Aric's fight was one of the main events and it was scheduled towards the end of the evening. The fight was unbelievable. The crowd was absolutely shocked by his abilities. One minute and twenty seconds into the fight, Aric won by a submission. He was the new Bantam Weight Champion for our state. We all were so excited for him!

The next day as we were traveling back home, Aric caught me by surprise. He said, "Oh yeah, I forgot to tell you about my dream the night before the weigh-in."

"What dream?" I asked.

"Chris visited me," said Aric. "He told me I was going to be fine and that I just needed to have more faith in myself."

I couldn't believe it. I was shocked! I told Aric how I had asked Chris for his help that very day. Needless to say, Aric was just as shocked as I was. We both realized that Chris had answered my prayers by helping Aric. I cried from happiness the whole way home. I was completely amazed at how well Chris was able to hear me and help from The Other Side.

Over the years I have realized how powerful Chris' presence really is. When he passed I was devastated, wondering how I would ever be able to live my life without him. Since then, however, Chris has taught me that he is there by my side whenever I need his help. He is still such a huge and important part of my life.

I cherish all the memories and experiences I had with him. He taught me what it is like to love, laugh and have a true friend. Any time I am missing him, I just talk to him and I know he hears me.

I know that my precious moments with Chris are not over, and there are many more to come. The saying that "love never dies" is so true. The mutual love we have for each other will never cease.

Although Chris' physical life was cut short, his energy lives on in a big way. Those of us who were fortunate enough to know him recognize what a great impact he has had on each of us. There really was no one else like him. I know he will continue to love me, make me laugh and be there for me.

I think the best gift I could give him is to be happy. One day when it is my time to cross over, I know he will be there to greet me, and I take great comfort in that.

Chris,

Thank you so much for always being there for me and also being there for my mom. You were such an important part of my life and I couldn't have asked for a better friend.

I still laugh when I think back to some of the amazing memories that we have together.

You already know what we shared and how I feel. But, in response to your last text and visits, I love you too, more than words could ever express.

Please don't worry about me like you did when you were alive. I am happy and healthy and I know that you know that now.

With your guidance and love, I promise you that I will live my life to my fullest potential, with you always in my heart! I miss you and love you!

Love,
Mandi Lane
Xoxoxo

P.S. I know you know this already, but I am a month away from graduating with my Bachelor's Degree in Graphic Design. Thank you for your faith in me!

14

Olivia's Story

Hide & Seek

Chris and Olivia, Balboa Bay Club October 2005

Chris was my brother and was fourteen years older than me. I have always felt his presence around me since his crossing, mostly when I am alone in my room and falling asleep. At those times I felt someone standing at the foot of my bed, but I was too scared to find out who it might be. What if it wasn't my brother? I would just pull the covers over my head and wait for the feeling to go away.

I had never had an ADC dream about Chris until recently. My dream was astoundingly clear and real. Chris came to me and told me he was always with me and watching out for me. He also said how much he loved me. Then he gave me a hug. I could feel his arms around me, the warmth and pressure, and I could smell him too. It was so weird. It was as if he were alive and standing there in person. I woke up still feeling his presence, the hug and the smell of him.

My mom took this picture on June 5, 2010 while I was cleaning my room. In it there is a rather large orb above my head. We both felt it was Chris' energy. It is approximately 17 inches in diameter when taken in reference to the picture on the wall behind it.

Talk'n To Grandpa

I've felt a little left out because everyone else seems to have had more experiences with Chris since the accident. I've only had that one visit from my brother, and I'm puzzled why he hasn't come to see me more often. I know I have been open to Spirit since I was a little girl. My dad and mom would catch me carrying on conversations when I was alone in my room. Other times I'd be in the back seat of the car talking away.

My dad's favorite story happened when I was six or seven and we were out trail riding in Idaho. We were riding alongside each other and suddenly my dad felt compelled to ask me if I had been talking to anyone lately. I said yes and he asked me if I knew who it was.

"It's Grandpa," I told him.

"Grandpa! Which Grandpa?" he asked.

I rolled my eyes and said, "Dad! I've been talking to *your* dad!"

"*My* dad? How do you know it was my dad? You never met him. He died before you were born," he exclaimed.

"Well, he's here now, sitting on the back of my horse!" I declared.

I was young, so I don't recall the incident too well, but I do know that I am always aware of the spirit world around me. My mom has taught me many things about Spirit and how incredible it is on The Other Side. She says we just drop our bodies when we die and nothing else is lost. I love listening to her stories, especially the stories about the hummingbirds—the one that came into the garage when she was sorting through my brother's things, the one that landed on her hand in the new house, and the one that took a ride on the broom in our Forever Home.

Circle Of Friends

In September of 2010 I had my own hummingbird experience. It was the beginning of my sophomore year of high school. In September it was customary for the student body to gather for prayer and recognition of the three seniors who were killed in a single car accident three years earlier.

At the end of the ceremony we all gathered in a circle on the lawn in front of the school. As we stood in silence, thoughts of my brother came to mind. It's hard not to think about him when reminded of someone else's death. All of a sudden, three hummingbirds appeared near a tree close to us. They swooped in above the crowd and hovered together in a small circle for about thirty seconds.

I glanced to my left and caught my friend, Kayli, staring right back at me, her mouth open in awe. We looked at each other and then back at the hummingbirds. We both knew what it meant. The three teens were there with us, watching us as we remembered them.

It was magical to see and I was glad my girlfriend had shared that moment with me. The sad thing was that no one else seemed to notice.

Most people just go on about their lives unaware of the magic that can happen at any moment.

When I got home after school I shared the story with my mom. She just smiled that knowing smile—you know the kind I mean—that *I told you so smile*, and went on about her day.

15

Barbara's Story

On The Wings Of Love

Chris loves to visit when I'm gardening. I have a garden angel with chimes, and over the last few years Chris checks in by sounding the chimes. Some days when there's no breeze at all, the chimes will sing and move. It's unbelievable. It's as if someone grabbed them and shook them. I always smile and say, "Hello Chris!"

My favorite experience with Chris occurred late in July of 2009. Kelly Wardell, my partner in life and Mandi's stepdad, was working in his welding shop. It was a very warm day, and he had his overhead 14-foot door open. He noticed a very small bird flying back and forth, circling the shop. He'd made several attempts to get the bird out of the shop, but the little bird wouldn't have any of it and just kept flying high up in the ceiling area.

Later that day when we were together, Kelly said he had to go back to his shop to get the little bird out, so I decided to join him and help with the rescue.

When we got to the shop we located the little guy on a ledge at the highest point of the ceiling. Setting up his twenty-two foot ladder, Kelly went straight for the bird, but it didn't move. Kelly reached out his hand for the capture and got no resistance; not a single feather flew.

Once he was off the ladder, Kelly and I went outside into the sunshine. Kelly thought it was a hummingbird, but he wasn't sure. We sat on the curb together and Kelly slowly opened his hand to release the little guy, but the bird surprised us by just sitting still.

Upon closer inspection we realized he was, in fact a hummingbird, but not like the ones that we'd ever seen in Idaho or in Wyoming where Kelly is from.

Holding out his hand where the bird was perched, Kelly removed his cell phone to take a couple pictures. The bird was so beautiful. His little eyes were wide open, looking at us for comfort and safety, as if he knew we were his friends.

After a good fifteen minutes, we talked about setting him on some bushes where he could hang out. Just then he flew off, over our heads and landed on the roof of the building next door. He sat on the edge looking down, as if to say, "Hello…" or, "Yes… this is Chris checking in!"

I looked at Kelly and said, "That had to be Chris." I could just feel it and knew it was him.

Later I looked up this bird in my bird book. He was a Costas Hummingbird. It said the Costas lived in California, Arizona, and Mexico during the winter months. The book said that southern Utah was as far north as the bird would go. Yet here we were farther north, in Idaho.

Chris,

Thank you for making the long trip to Idaho. We are all looking forward to your next visit. I love and miss you!

Barb Patterson

16

Shelly's Story

Happy Valentine's Day

Valentine's Day 2011

During the month of February 2011, as I mentioned previously, I found myself in a state of deep depression. It started in the middle of January as it had every year since Chris had crossed over, and as the anniversary of his accident approached. The sadness usually lasted several weeks, but this time it was different. Writing the book had opened wounds that I realized would never heal. The pain was overwhelming and I just didn't want to be here anymore.

I had sunk to a new low, didn't leave the house, and barely felt like showering. If I could get my daughter, Olivia, to stop by the grocery store or a fast food restaurant on her way home from school, I knew she would at least have something to eat for dinner. I honestly wasn't up to preparing a meal for her, although without fail, every day of her life I have made her school lunch and had continued to do so during this time. I always felt it was important to say goodbye to her as she left for school each day.

It was a really dark time for me. Some days I wouldn't even take pictures of the orbs around the house as had become my custom over the past two years. It always filled me with joy, knowing they were there. In fact, Olivia would often tease me and say that I loved the orbs more than I loved her.

That's not true, of course, but they are infinitely more entertaining to watch as they zoom around the room illuminated by the infrared light on my camera. I usually laugh and tease them, and in return they've given me some beautiful pictures.

Sometimes I may get a small one hiding quietly by the ceiling or resting with my two dogs on their chair. Other times I would see a larger, intricately detailed Light Being hovering in mid-air, watching me in silence, standing guard. Then of course, the entire gang would show up and there would be hundreds in my kitchen, living room or bedroom. They each have their own individual markings and they come in a vast variety of sizes.

The shape is always the same beautiful circle. Some have a circle within a circle while others have bumps, knobs, tracks or holes in their interiors. You may see magnificent coronas or radiant colors and some even have faces.

I've noticed they follow me even when I travel; I've photographed them in my hotel room, in the car and on the airplane. I was photographed with orbs while skydiving in a wind tunnel at 130 mph, more proof that they are *not* dust particles as many skeptics claim. They love to have me take their picture. Sometimes I have to ask them to stay out of the picture because I actually need one without them!

I truly feel my son is connected with the orbs. As I mentioned previously, I believe that many of them are our essence: what we are when we are out of body.

On the night of February 14, 2011, I took several shots just for the heck of it. My heart really wasn't into it as I sat by myself watching TV and moping, but during the past few weeks the table lamp near the bar had started to flicker. I thought maybe Chris was trying to get my attention so I picked up my camera.

Several days later, when I finally recovered my interest

in the orbs and the photos I'd taken of them, I scrolled back through the more recent ones and noticed a bright pink orb by my angel in the living room, just a few feet away from the flickering lamp.

Colored orbs are more infrequent in pictures. I looked at the date stamp on the digital photo. It was Valentine's Day.

Chris must have felt my sorrow and wanted to send me some love. The orb near the angel was significant to me because I always see her as the Angel of Love and Protection for my house. She brings peace and tranquility to my surroundings and when I think of her, I think of my son in Heaven. I've placed the cropped color photo of the angel and orb on the back cover of this book. It can also be found on my website miraclemessenger.com along with all the other photos in this book.

Two books, *The Orb Project*, by Miceal Ledwith, D.D., LL.D. and Klaus Heineman, Ph.D., and *Orbs: Their Mission and Message of Hope*, by Klaus Heineman, Ph.D. and Gundi Heineman, give the reader great insight into this relatively new field.

Klaus Heineman holds a Ph.D. in experimental physics. Over the years he has worked in materials science research at NASA and UCLA, and as a research professor at Stanford University. In his latest book, *Orbs: Their Mission and Message of Hope*, he states, "It is our position, then, that orbs appear in meaningful places in photographs, and not haphazardly; it is because they are there by design."

Some people may contend that orbs are nothing more than dust particles in the air, and depending on the picture, that may be true. However, according to Miceal Ledwith, D.D., LL.D., coauthor of *The Orb Project*, "A careful analysis of the data collected in this study clearly shows that the orb phenomenon is real and cannot be explained away by the myriad suggestions that have been produced to account for it, such as raindrops or fog, dust particles or pollen in the air, lens flare, bokeh, or digital processing errors."

Orbs exist. I have physically seen and interacted with them. They come when I summon them and they follow me when I travel. Below is a cropped photo of my nephew taken during Christmas 2010. He is in the process of trying to capture a "sputnik," as I lovingly refer to that particular type of orb. Notice the complete look of joy and excitement on his face. A larger one is behind his head. In the original photo there were approximately twenty orbs.

In 2009, I took Olivia and her friends to Disneyland for her fifteenth birthday. It was the first time I'd been there since the fall of 2005 when my mother had arranged a family get-together with Chris, Logan and the rest of the family.

It was difficult for me to return to this place that held such sweet memories of that time when Chris was still with us in physical body.

During the drive, I found myself becoming melancholy.

I tried not to let Olivia notice, and as we settled into our rooms I took a few pictures. I was half dreading the visit to the California Adventure Park the following day because Chris, Logan, Olivia and I had stopped on the bridge to take a family picture. The memories were overwhelming and I needed some levity interjected into the situation, fast.

The girls started laughing and hugging and bouncing off the beds and in one of the pictures I caught Olivia and her friend in a Happy Birthday hug. It wasn't until I reviewed the photos a few minutes later that I noticed a large orb, in the open doorway on the balcony, above and behind the girls. We could all clearly see a smiling bear face in the orb. It made me smile and lightened my heart. I totally felt that my son had made that happen!

17

Kristin's Story

Oh Child Of Mine

Chris and Kristin Fall 1986

I have always had an incredibly deep connection with my brother, Chris. My mother told me that from Day One she knew he and I were "two souls created from the same mold," or, she would say, "twins born four years apart!"

She used to joke that she named my brother "Chris" and me "Kristin" so she could call us for dinner at the same time. "Chris—Tin! It's time for dinner!" she would yell. Although we both found this trick annoying, we always came running side by side.

Together we faced the world. When things got scary we stuck together. When no one else understood us we understood each other. As children we would often snuggle up under the covers and talk about life and how we felt that we had incarnated on this earth for a very important mission; a mission to help save the planet, to help raise the level of consciousness of the people on this earth and usher in the new age of love and compassion.

I remember looking at him as a little girl and knowing that we came from the same place somewhere deep within the universe and that together we would accomplish our assignment. With every ounce of my being, I knew that he and I came here together for a very important cause and that together we would complete it.

I never spoke to others about our plans, our dreams, or our connection. It never needed discussing. Our love for each other went unspoken. A deep understanding bridged our hearts and I always knew that no matter what, we had each other.

However, of all the things Chris and I did share, there was one thing I had kept to myself. This one thing I had never told anyone, because even as a child I knew it was unusual.

Although I loved my brother dearly, for as long as I can remember, I couldn't understand why I came into this world as his sister and not his mother. I felt that God had done a good job of putting us in the same family, but somehow things got a little mixed up and I became his sister instead of his mom.

For many years I explained away my thoughts and suppressed these strange feelings. In an attempt to make sense of it all, I told myself that I only felt this way because I loved him so much and understood him so well.

As the years went by and he and I grew into young adults, our plans to make a difference in this world started to form.

We both decided that film would be the avenue we would take to reach massive amounts of people. Together we went to schools in Texas and studied film and photography. I was enrolled at Southern Methodist University and Chris at the Dallas Art Institute. I stayed in Dallas for two years until I decided a school in northern California would suit me better. Following my lead, Chris moved to southern California shortly after I left Texas, to pursue his career in film making.

Life seemed perfect in the days prior to my brother's crossing. He and I were both living in California, preparing to live our dreams and complete the mission we had talked about since childhood. We couldn't wait to start traveling and making documentaries together that exposed important global issues. Our films would help bring people together and create necessary change for a world filled with love.

Three days before his death I remember hearing a voice say to me, "Enjoy it while it lasts." I didn't understand the meaning of these words until the morning of February 4 when I received the phone call from my mother.

The day my brother died, I died too. Everything I had believed in and loved with my entire soul was gone in an instant. Every day after school for the first year I lay in the dark in the bathtub drinking beer and crying until I couldn't cry any more. I seriously contemplated joining my brother on The Other Side. Over and over again I said to him, "Why wasn't I on the back of that motorcycle that night with you? This was not part of the plan! We have a job to do down here. How could you just abandon me like this? What am I supposed to do now?"

The only life I knew was life with my brother, Chris by

my side. How could I live without him? How could I live without my other half? My twin flame? My partner in crime? My best friend? I didn't want to live any more. I felt if he had bailed out on his part of the deal by dying before we completed our mission, then I wanted to join him.

A few months after Chris died, I started having ADC's with him. One night in particular, as I lay sleeping, I found myself at a pool with my brother and his son, Logan. As I stood there watching them play in the sunshine and the water, Chris stood up and walked towards me.

When he reached me he put both of his hands on my shoulders, looked me straight in the eyes and continued to repeat, "Kristin, I'm coming back! Tell Mom that I'm coming back. When you wake up, don't forget that I've told you I AM coming back! Make sure you tell Mom, okay?"

Each time he repeated this he shook my shoulders intensely to make sure I understood the importance of his message. After hearing this over and over again I pushed his hands off me and told him, "All right, all right, okay! I get the message! You can stop shaking me now. I'll make sure I tell Mom. I promise I'll remember."

When I awoke, I knew I had just met with my brother in an after-death communication. The clarity and energy of my encounter with him left no doubt in my mind that my brother planned to return to this earth. Needless to say, I called my mom first thing in the morning and told her about my dream.

I felt so grateful to have seen him again; to have touched his skin, looked into his eyes, seen his smile, and to have heard him tell me of his plans to return.

Later that night when I got into the tub, I cracked open a beer and felt myself slipping into my same nightly routine of crying and drinking. Just as the first tears started to fill my eyes, a sudden bolt of what felt like lightning shot through my body. In the same instant a light bulb went off in my head.

I sat straight up in the tub and heard my brother's voice say to me, "Kristin, I'm coming back, and now you *can* be my mother."

These words brought my world to a screeching halt. Time stood still. The tears stopped. The lump in my throat softened, and everything I had questioned, doubted, cried about, feared and hated since his death suddenly disappeared. Love, hope, light, and excitement replaced them.

That moment changed the course of my life. It made me realize that Chris' death had been a part of the plan.

Instantly, all the thoughts I'd had about being his mother when I was a child made perfect sense. At last I understood. My life turned around. I had something to look forward to. I finished college with honors, and with the help and guidance from my brother on The Other Side, I started EQ Heavenly Hands, my own sports therapy business for horses and their riders.

For the first time in years I felt happy again. I told my mother about the after-death communication dream and that Chris wanted her to know that he was coming back—but I never told her or anyone else about what he told *me* that night. I kept that between us. Although I knew in my heart he had come to me in my sleep and had spoken to me about how he planned to return, I never wanted to share that with anyone.

As the years passed, I felt a deeper urge to take time off so I could really connect with my own spirit. I felt I needed to get away from work and school and take time to fully heal the deepest parts of my soul.

Even though my brother's words allowed me to keep living and to move forward, I had not taken time off since his death to fully process everything that had happened in my life since his crossing.

I felt that my brother was encouraging me to go through the Sedona Intensive program, just as he had.

Packing my bags, I headed for Sedona, Arizona where I planned to spend a week completing Albert Gaulden's program.

On the fifth day of the program I felt my brother's presence more than ever. I felt he wanted to remind me that he still planned to reincarnate and that he would be my son. At this point it had been three years since he'd first told me of his plans and I had never shared my experiences concerning this matter with a single soul. I didn't care to hear others' opinions about it, nor did I care to hear the ridicule others may have. It is such a taboo topic and sadly, I have never told most of my friends about my after-life experiences. In my heart, I know that an unbreakable bond exists between my brother and me and I didn't need anyone else to validate my experiences with him.

However, after three years of keeping this inside of me, I began to feel a little crazy. I questioned myself and my experiences with Chris. Were my feelings about his return real or not? Did my brother actually communicate with me from The Other Side, or have I completely lost my mind? All of these questions raced through my mind as I drove to my last meeting that afternoon at Albert's office.

I tried to analyze my own thoughts and even started to question my sanity. Finally I said firmly out loud, "Okay, Chris. I feel like I can hear you loud and clear. I feel like you're telling me that you're coming back and that you are coming back through me. However, I also feel like a total nut case at this point because this has been going on for three years. If you are really there, if you are really saying these things to me, I need some proof. I need to know that beyond a shadow of a doubt, all of this is real and that you *are* coming back. So, if you're out there and you can hear me, make this happen."

After saying this out loud I released it from my heart. I figured if Chris had just heard my request he would smack me in the face with the answer. If not, then I would need to drop it and force myself to stop having thoughts about his return.

As I pulled into Albert's driveway, I let my request to my brother drift from my mind and I focused on the session at hand. Once I completed my hour long session, I collected my belongings, thanked Albert for everything he had helped me with throughout the week, and headed towards the door. As I opened the door to walk out, Albert, who was sitting in his chair behind his desk, swiveled around and with a certain amount of urgency, said, "Kristin! Wait! Come back! I have to tell you something!"

Caught off guard I took a few steps backwards, peeked around the corner, raised an eyebrow and said, "Yes? What is it?"

"I have something important to tell you," Albert said, 'but I don't want it to freak you out. I'm getting a message from Chris and he's telling me that it's really important that I tell you, but you have to promise me you won't get scared."

At this point I could feel the blood starting to drain from my face. I knew that Albert had the ability to work as a medium and communicate with The Other Side, so that didn't scare me—but nothing could have prepared me for the bombshell he was going to drop.

He sat up, looked me straight in the eye and said, "Chris is telling me that he wants you to know that he's coming back, and that he is going to be your son…"

Like a cartoon in the movies, my jaw fell to the floor, my knees buckled beneath me, and I burst into tears. Suddenly, the silent, mystical world I had kept all to myself from childhood had became a reality. Within an hour of asking my brother to give me an answer, he had communicated with me through Albert and reassured me that what I had heard for the past three years was real. What I had felt as a child was real. Never in my life have I experienced a moment of such purity, truth, and validation. No one in the entire world knew about the conversations I'd had with my brother and about his plans to reincarnate as my son. Yet one hour after my request for validation, Chris smacked me in the face with an answer he had been telling me all along.

I do not know when Chris will return to this world, but I do know that when he does, he will move mountains.

I love you Beanie, and I cannot wait to see you again.
Love always,
Your Dills

We Are Not Alone

Chris and Shelly, Lake Tahoe 2001

    I have experienced a life filled with surprises mixed with great joy and very deep sorrows. It has made me who I am and I am stronger, more loving and more forgiving as a result of these experiences.

    We are not alone on this spinning planet in this vast universe. There is love all around us. We are all the same spark of brilliant white light, covered by individual canvasses on which we paint a picture of our lives. It is this beautiful light that we must look to uncover in every person we meet.

    We live with the illusion that we are separate from God and each other when in fact we are all a drop in the same bucket.

    Following is a poem I wrote for my son's ceremony with a little help from my friend, Tomi Fratto. For twenty years, Tomi served as my mother's secretary. She watched Chris grow up and bring his own son into the world.

Believe

Sadness does not dwell in Heaven
or in hearts that understand
Our soul is filled with many lessons
in our life as mortal man
We pass this way not once, but many,
until we learn that love's divine
Forgiveness opens every door
and selflessness is sublime

Do not weep your loved one's crossing,
but wish them joy and peace
We each trusted God's great plan
when we chose our time to leave
The journey back to Heaven
is quicker than we know
For death is not an ending,
but a transition for the soul

My spirit remembers many things
my mind now comprehends
A guiding light and warm embrace
of a true and loving friend
All these things wait for us
through the open door
Lift the veil and you shall see
where all our souls have soared

My son has gone before me,
there is little sadness here
My heart is filled to bursting
with pure love and not with fear
Sweet energy brings me comfort
and I feel a welcome bliss
An angel's here beside me
and I have no doubt it's Chris

I can't explain the things I know
that in my heart are true
A memory of a distant place,
a golden light and you
Please live each day in joy and love
so you're ready when you leave
Heaven's just a breath away
if you'd only just believe…

VMH
6/2006

About The Author

Virginia Michelle "Shelly" Hummel is the mother of four children, one of whom, Christopher, was killed in a motorcycle accident in February 2006. She is also the proud grandmother of Chris' ten-year-old son, Logan.

Shelly is a devoted student of spirituality and metaphysics and a Certified Light Therapist. She currently lives in Southern California.

Her website is www.miraclemessenger.com

For speaking engagements on "Light Beings-Our Divine Connection to The Other Side" please contact her at author@miraclemessenger.com

Coming in 2012, *Miracle Messengers: Orbs and Light Beings-Our Divine Connection to The Other Side.*

Bibliography

Bach, Richard D. and Parrish-Bach, Leslie, *Jonathan Livingston Seagull* from Richard D. Bach, ©1970. All rights reserved. Avon Books, a division of the Hearst Corporation. Published by arrangment with The Macmillan Company

Guggenheim Bill & Judy, *Hello From Heaven!* ©1995 The ADC Project, P.O. Box 916070, Longwood, FL 32791 www.after-death.com

Heineman, Klaus, and Heineman, Gundi *Orbs: Their Mission and Messages of Hope* (Hay House, Inc., 2010, Carlsbad, CA)

Ledwith, Miceal, and Heineman, Klaus, *The Orb Project* (Atria Books, division of Simon and Schuster, 2007, New York, NY)

Virtue, Doreen, *Archangels & Ascended Masters: A Guide to Working and Healing with Divinities and Deities.* (Hay House, Inc., 2005, Carlsbad, CA)